HowE
to Study Skills

101 Tips to Learn How to Study Effectively, Improve Your Grades, and Become a Better Student

HowExpert with Sarah Fantinel

For more tips related to this topic, visit HowExpert.com/studyskills.

Recommended Resources

- HowExpert.com – Quick 'How To' Guides on All Topics from A to Z by Everyday Experts.
- HowExpert.com/free – Free HowExpert Email Newsletter.
- HowExpert.com/books – HowExpert Books
- HowExpert.com/courses – HowExpert Courses
- HowExpert.com/clothing – HowExpert Clothing
- HowExpert.com/membership – HowExpert Membership Site
- HowExpert.com/affiliates – HowExpert Affiliate Program
- HowExpert.com/jobs – HowExpert Jobs
- HowExpert.com/writers – Write About Your #1 Passion/Knowledge/Expertise & Become a HowExpert Author.
- HowExpert.com/resources – Additional HowExpert Recommended Resources
- YouTube.com/HowExpert – Subscribe to HowExpert YouTube.
- Instagram.com/HowExpert – Follow HowExpert on Instagram.
- Facebook.com/HowExpert – Follow HowExpert on Facebook.

Publisher's Foreword

Dear HowExpert Reader,

HowExpert publishes quick 'how to' guides on all topics from A to Z by everyday experts.

At HowExpert, our mission is to discover, empower, and maximize everyday people's talents to ultimately make a positive impact in the world for all topics from A to Z...one everyday expert at a time!

All of our HowExpert guides are written by everyday people just like you and me, who have a passion, knowledge, and expertise for a specific topic.

We take great pride in selecting everyday experts who have a passion, real-life experience in a topic, and excellent writing skills to teach you about the topic you are also passionate about and eager to learn.

We hope you get a lot of value from our HowExpert guides, and it can make a positive impact on your life in some way. All of our readers, including you, help us continue living our mission of positively impacting the world for all spheres of influences from A to Z.

If you enjoyed one of our HowExpert guides, then please take a moment to send us your feedback from wherever you got this book.

Thank you, and we wish you all the best in all aspects of life.

Sincerely,

BJ Min
Founder & Publisher of HowExpert
HowExpert.com

PS...If you are also interested in becoming a HowExpert author, then please visit our website at HowExpert.com/writers. Thank you & again, all the best!

COPYRIGHT, LEGAL NOTICE AND DISCLAIMER:

Table of Contents

Chapter 1: Introduction

Amanda exemplified many qualities people generally consider necessary for a good student: organization, attendance, intelligence. Yet, she was struggling to pass algebra when her friends seemed to have no problem. Amanda had never struggled in school before. She wasn't happy with her grade. She knew she could do better, and she really wanted to. After struggling through most of the school year, Amanda finally came to me.

Zach had not been in school for over 40 years, and his grades when he was in school last time were not something that he was proud of. He came back to finish his degree and finally achieve his dream of being an elementary school teacher, preferably teaching second grade, but he was never very good at school. His grades this time weren't much better, and with the comprehensive teacher test looming, Zach worried that he would not be able to graduate again. With nowhere else to turn, Zach came to me.

I am a tutor. While I have my academic focuses, my specialization is with students who are struggling in the classroom. Academic success is not as easy as the movies make it out to be. I know this because I have spent years helping both myself and others work their way through their education and towards their personal goals. I help students build the skills they need to succeed and teach them how to apply those skills to other classes and life. School is the preparation ground for life, so I help those struggling with school, whether they be completely drowning or just needing a little focused attention.

My goal for this book is to give you access to the same knowledge and support that I give my students. Education is one of the most important things that a person can pursue, and there is no reason that you can't have the support you need to succeed. Of course, success takes a lot of work; I have met very few students who are able to thrive in the long term who do not put in significant amounts of work. This book will guide you through a whole class, from the first day to the last, giving you advice and lessons to remember as you work towards your goals. If you put in the work now, you will set yourself up for success.

The first chapter focuses on the classroom itself. Academic success begins and ends here, so it's the perfect place to start. Walk into the first day prepared: have your planner and all your materials ready and with you. Know what class you are going to, and if there is anything you can read in advance (like a syllabus or the introduction to your textbook), you should do so.

Once you get to class, try to sit in the first couple of rows, although anywhere in the T-zone is good. Look around and try to make a couple of friends who seem to be good students, like you. These people can serve as your study buddies and safety net throughout the class. As the class proceeds, ask your teacher questions. Don't interrupt the lesson, but when your teacher calls for questions, you should ask about whatever you are unsure of. If you are uncomfortable speaking in front of everyone, ask your teacher after class. Your education is essential, so you should chase it.

As the lessons begin, you should take notes. I usually suggest writing your notes by hand if possible because your brain remembers more of what you write than what you type. As you are writing your entries in your notebook, organize them, so they are easier to read later. It takes more work during class, but studying and learning are easier later if you manage your notes while taking them.

The second chapter focuses on the art of studying. It is where most people will focus their anxiety and attempts at self-improvement, and for a good reason. Without the dedicated practice that studying allows, people cannot learn new material effectively. A lot of the study skills I teach my students revolve around how the brain handles repetition. Therefore, to have effective study sessions, I suggest that my students pick a specific area or two and designate them as study spaces. For me, these spaces have been a particular seat in my kitchen, a certain table in the back of the library, and my favorite coffee shop. Having a specific location helps your brain settle into the rhythm of studying, making it easier for you to focus on what you are learning.

As you plan your study sessions, you should also consider how you need to manage your time. Pull out your planner and set aside a couple of hours every day to devote to your studying. If possible, try to be consistent: study at the same time every day. Of course, the actual art of studying looks different for everyone and every subject. I usually advise using flashcards for things that need to simply be memorized (such as vocabulary words and historical dates). I suggest practice problems for subjects like math, which can usually be found easily on the

Internet. I also advise students to read over their notes right before they go to bed because their brain will process them while they sleep. All studying techniques require you to put in some repetitious work, but studying in this way helps you to truly learn the material and achieve your academic goals.

The third chapter focuses on writing essays and papers. I have helped many students learn how to write reports, and a good paper is often a non-negotiable part of a good grade. The first step to writing a good essay is knowing what you are writing about. Sometimes your teacher will give you a topic; sometimes, your teacher will tell you to pick a topic. Either way, you need to know what you are writing about because your topic will drive your research. Start your research broadly. I usually recommend having two more sources than the required page count of your paper, but this is not a hard and fast rule. Read deeply and widely, and make a note of where you find quotations and specific information. You will need this later when you cite your sources.

Once you have completed your research, write out your thesis. A thesis is the central argument of your paper, and all good papers have one. Then outline your essay. Note what each paragraph will be about, and place some of your research into your outline, so you remember where you wanted to use your evidence. At this point, now that you have a thesis and a researched outline, you can write your paper. This first draft is your rough draft, so it doesn't have to be perfect. You can make your essay better during the revision and editing stages. Revising is when you change the content of your paper. It can be rewriting paragraphs or strengthening a sentence. Editing is when you verify your report is technically accurate by checking your spelling and grammar.

Once you have finished revising and editing, read over your paper once more for continuity.

Remember, writing good papers takes time. There is no set amount of time for writing an essay, but for your first one, plan for two weeks of work, including research. As you become more comfortable writing papers, you will learn how long you need to complete each piece well. Plan out your research and writing time just like you plan out your studying time. If you put in the work, you will set yourself up to write a successful paper.

The fourth chapter focuses on taking tests. Tests are often a source of anxiety for students, but I believe that tests do not need to be stressful with the proper test-taking tools and the right preparations. Instead, tests are an opportunity to prove that you know your stuff. Tests are where you demonstrate that you have achieved your academic goals. Many of the students I work with have told me that taking tests is stressful. They read a question and panic because they don't immediately know the answer. It usually spirals out and affects their ability to perform on the entire test, not just on that one question. The first lesson I teach my students is to breathe while they take their tests. Panicking restricts your breathing usually, limiting the amount of oxygen that goes to your brain because the oxygen is being diverted elsewhere. Taking a deep breath helps. The next lesson is to read the question carefully. Make sure you know what exactly it is asking for. If you are still stuck at this point, write down everything you know about this question or problem. It is especially helpful in math and science, but it can be used in all disciplines. Writing everything you do know helps you focus on what you do not. Usually, my students find that writing what they understand helps them realize they already know the answer.

There are many different types of tests, and every kind of test has its own tips. On multiple-choice tests, if you do not know the answer, use the answer choices to help you. Eliminate what is obviously wrong. Guess and check the answers with the problem. On essay tests, make sure you know what the question is asking and structure your thesis with as many keywords from the question as possible. Jot down a quick outline to make sure you stay on topic, and then write. Don't worry about your essay being perfect; your teacher is not expecting perfection. On matching tests, use the answers to help you figure out any questions you don't know. Treat matching tests like multiple-choice tests, only with more options to sort through. On true-false tests, read each statement carefully. The whole statement is false if even one part is false. On short answer tests, treat each open question as a tiny essay test. Understand what the question is asking, and only answer that question. If your short answer test has "fill in the blank" and you cannot remember the correct term, do not leave it blank. Instead, write down everything you do remember about that term. The key to taking tests well is to demonstrate how prepared and knowledgeable you are. You won't be perfect, but tests are one of the areas where you can display the hard work you have put into achieving academic success.

The fifth chapter focuses on the other projects that come along in the academic environment. These are things like presentations, speeches, and group work. All these projects come with their struggles and rewards, and I want you to be as prepared as possible. When you are crafting a presentation, try to think about it as a verbal essay. You have a main point you are trying to make (a thesis), so everything in the presentation should support that central thesis. Organize your thoughts into distinctive categories, and move logically from one to the next. Giving a good presentation depends upon you doing the necessary work and preparation ahead of time.

If your presentation has a visual component (like a PowerPoint), treat your visual component as a tool to help you, not as a stand-alone item that can give your presentation without you. Use ten words or fewer per slide, although this is not a hard and fast rule, and pick pictures that support what you are saying. If you are using a poster, you can use complete sentences, but try to use more images and charts than paragraphs. Have clear structures within your posters, such as directional arrows or color blocks, to help your audience move through your poster with ease. The visual component of your presentation should help your audience better understand what you are presenting and help your audience pay more attention to you. As you are giving your oral presentation, remember to breathe. Many people experience stage fright in some way or another, so you are not alone. The only way to overcome stage fright is to confront it by talking in front of other people repeatedly. Practice your presentation in front of people you trust so that you can build your confidence. Practice standing up straight and acting like you are confident. As you give your presentation itself, look at people's ears, nose, or forehead if you cannot bring yourself to look them in the eyes. Remind yourself that you have practiced this before, but don't expect perfection. I have never seen or given a perfect presentation, but I have seen and given many good ones.

There are other projects that arise in the academic environment, and one of the most dreaded is the group project. Group projects usually are sources of conflict because there is an unequal distribution of responsibility and an unwillingness to collaborate. Of course, you cannot produce a successful group project on your own. All you can do is facilitate the necessary environment for a successful group project and hope that your group mates will also encourage a collaborative environment. To better ensure equal distribution of responsibility, write down each aspect of the project and who will be responsible for what. It leads to fewer conflicts later on. Also, make sure that any dispute in the group does not come from you. Do not attempt to undermine anyone else's work, and do your work to the best of your ability. If your group project is falling apart, reach out to your teacher. Your teacher may or may not know what is happening in your group but can usually offer advice, assistance, or assurance of equitable grades. However, I have only had a few groups that have needed that drastic of a solution. Most group projects can be managed well with honest collaboration and healthy conflict management. Like every other relationship you're in, group projects take work, but that work often leads to success.

The sixth chapter covers some of the frequently asked questions that I don't answer in the first five chapters.

This section will cover topics such as staying healthy, studying online, and avoiding procrastination. The foundation of good study skills is your health; you should never sacrifice your health and wellbeing for a grade. That means that you need to take time to get enough sleep (experts recommend at least 8 hours and sometimes more), that you need to take time to eat nutritious food, and that you need to try to meet your emotional needs adequately. Emotional needs can be met in various ways: spending time with friends, enjoying a movie, exercising, talking with a therapist, engaging in creative expression, etc. If you find that your schoolwork is dominating your life to the point that you are not healthy, re-evaluate your expectations for yourself. Once you have your priorities straightened back out, you will feel less stressed and more focused.

As technology continues to develop, we see a shift towards online education. Online classes allow for more flexibility, but they do not offer the same access to teachers or the structure that traditional courses provide. To compensate for this, you need to be self-motivated and dedicated to keeping your study schedule. Planning out specific study times is more important than ever in an increasingly virtual world. Keep to your study schedule as strictly as you keep to your work schedule. You wouldn't just skip a day of work, so don't just skip a study session. Many teachers are available for questions via email, so use that. Don't be self-conscious about sending too many emails; if you were in a traditional classroom, you would ask and listen to these questions there. Recently, however, I have helped a few students who are taking online classes with non-responsive teachers. It is frustrating. In the case of non-responsive teachers, I usually suggest that my students review the material again. If the answer is not there or is unclear, then use a search engine to pull up videos and articles that discuss whatever you are confused about. Studying online sometimes means you end up teaching yourself, so I say that you should use all the resources that studying online provides. You might just be surprised how many people are waiting to help you.

This sixth chapter will also discuss procrastination. In my experience, procrastination has very little to do with laziness and a great deal to do with anxiety and stress. Procrastination is a form of self-sabotage and usually comes from a fear of failure. The thought process is generally along the lines of 'if I don't do this assignment, then I can't fail at it.' I understand the anxiety of procrastination, and I have experienced how difficult it is to overcome it. When my students come to me for help with overcoming procrastination, the first thing I do is tell them they have already taken the first step: build a support system. Ask two or three people you trust to keep you accountable for your work. Your support system will give you the gentle push you need to keep yourself on schedule. The next step is to break the assignment into achievable pieces with personal due dates. Focus only upon the attainable part, and you will find that it is easier to finish the small goal if you are not stressing about the large goal. Finally, give yourself breaks. Some people procrastinate because they are tired but won't allow themselves to rest. Procrastination is one of the body's ways of reclaiming the rest it desperately needs. When you find yourself staring blankly at the book, unable to make yourself read another word, then stop for the night. Trying to force yourself through is not healthy and only creates more stress and self-loathing. You have been studying correctly because you've read this far and put these tips and lessons into practice; therefore, all you have left to do is beat the mind game that is procrastination.

I hope you find this book, with my tips and advice, to be as helpful in your endeavors as my students have found it. In all my years of tutoring, a wide variety of students have come to me for help reaching their academic goals. The students who followed my advice and put in the work saw success. If you follow my advice and you do the work I suggest, then I am confident that you, too, can be successful.

Chapter 2: It All Starts in the Classroom

One of the secrets to improving your grades and building the habits you need to become an excellent student starts in the classroom. It is where you have access to an expert in the field, whether it's molecular biology or US history, or band. It is where you have the opportunity to start, continue, and enhance the learning process. True learning rarely happens in isolation, so the first thing you need to do is prepare to step into the classroom.

Section 1: Pre-class Preparations

Some of the big problems that plague students come from a lack of preparation before classes start. Feeling overwhelmed and discombobulated in the last few weeks of a course can usually be traced back to a lack of preparation in the first few weeks of class. To nip some of these problems in the bud, let's take the time now to prepare for later. Your future self will thank you.

Organize Your Life

Your life does not have to be perfect for you to improve your grades. I've never known anyone who had an ideal life, but I have known and helped many students with imperfect lives improve their grades.

The first thing you need to do is corral the chaos of life, and that means establishing some method of organization. Having an organization method allows you to prepare for what is coming, which is one of the most beneficial study skills. It's harder to miss assignments (which instantly kills your grade, by the way) when you have them all written down together in an organized manner. Some people do this by running to-do lists. Some people stick to a strict schedule every day. I've found that keeping a planner is the best way to keep me organized.

Lesson 1: Find a planner you like and use it.

Your planner can be as fancy or as simple as you like. It can even be electronic. I tutored one student who prefers to draw her own planner every week. I tutored other students who use a free basic school planner. Whatever you choose, this is how I usually recommend students use their planners.

1. Write down your class times, work hours, and all other appointments you can't move (such as doctor's appointments, club meetings, and date nights.) Color coding your classes and other commitments make this fun.
2. Write in all the due dates for all your assignments in all your classes. If your teacher has a syllabus (see the next section), copy them down from the syllabus. If not, write them down as you learn about them. Either way, knowing when everything is due helps you prepare for it.
3. Use the remaining open time in your planner to plan out key studying times and objectives. It can be done on a weekly basis because, let's face it; life is unpredictable.

Lesson 2: Plan time for self-care.

As you are working on getting organized, don't forget to plan some time for fun and relaxation. Some people call this self-care, and it's essential for your emotional and mental wellbeing. I have met many struggling students because they haven't gotten a good night's sleep for weeks. They haven't planned time to hang out with friends or take care of themselves, sabotaging their attempts to become better students. Take a few hours off on a Saturday evening to watch a movie with your best friend. Make time for a workout during the week. Listen to your body; it will tell you when it desperately needs a breather.

Read the Syllabus—It Might Save Your Life

If your teacher has one, you should read your syllabus as soon as you get it. I've had teachers who planned their whole class down to the class meeting and daily homework assignments before the first day of school. But I've also had teachers who didn't have a syllabus until three weeks into a three-month class, and I've had teachers who never had one.

Lesson 3: A syllabus is your preview for the whole class.

A syllabus is a document that expresses the expectations of the classroom (which tend to be standard: be nice to people, show up, don't plagiarize, etc.) and lists the assignments of the class with their due dates. This latter section is the most crucial part of the syllabus, so you should pay extra close attention to it.

If your teacher does not have a formal syllabus (and some don't, especially in middle school and high school), they will most likely have due dates to write on the board or tell you during class. You should definitely pay attention to this. It serves as an abstract guide for the course and will help you well if you take the time to notice it.

However, you acquire your due dates, write them down in the planner we set up a couple of lessons ago. Once you have all your dates in, you can start planning out your study sessions (we'll go over this in more detail later).

Acquire Your Supplies

When Zach first came in for tutoring, he was severely failing his class. He was confused about why he was failing; he found the course interesting and liked his teacher. However, when I asked him to get out his notes, he said he didn't even have a notebook because he was an auditory learner. He could remember anything after hearing it once. (Actually, as a few of my questions about his last class meeting revealed, he couldn't.)

Lesson 4: Regardless of your learning style, you need a notebook for class.

In my time as a student and as a tutor, I have found that, generally, the human brain doesn't work like Zach thought it did. We need to hear things many times to remember them, and teachers don't tend to repeat themselves that often. So, to compensate, before you even go to class, make sure you have all the materials you need. You will need a notebook for notes. I recommend physical paper and a writing utensil (pen, pencil, completely up to you).

Lesson 5: Handwrite your notes during class.

Handwriting your notes increases memory retention compared to typing your notes, so give yourself a head start. Write your notes on paper if your handwriting is remotely legible.

Of course, I've met students who do not have legible handwriting, and they type their notes. It is completely fine. If you choose to go this route, make sure your electronic device is fully charged and in operational order. The last thing you want to do is get to class with a dead laptop.

Lesson 6: Organization decreases stress and increases success.

While you are gathering supplies, get your textbooks and whatever organizational device you will use to corral your class papers. I use a three-ring binder for most classes because it easily allows me to move pages around as I need to. Folders are also viable options, especially if the course is light on papers. Everyone likes something different; just make sure to choose something that works for you. The most important part is that you can find your papers and notes the moment you need them.

Once Zach got his school supplies and began taking notes, his test grades improved dramatically. Even auditory learners need the right supplies to achieve academic success. As a result of him finally getting the supplies he needed, he was able to save his grade and his GPA. When the next semester rolled around, he stepped into his classes fully prepared to be successful with a notebook in hand.

Actively Read Your Class Materials

If your teacher has required readings before class starts or before a class meeting, you should actively read those.

Lesson 7: Use active reading strategies on class readings.

Active reading is an interactive reading style that helps you engage with and remember what you've read. It includes highlighting key points, commenting in the margins, asking questions about the text, and summarizing key passages.

> Highlighting should be used only on key points; highlighting is like shining a spotlight on the essential parts or the main ideas. If there is too much highlighting, it's challenging to pick out what you need. Nonfiction authors usually state their main idea in the first or last sentence of a paragraph, so this will probably be where you highlight most in nonfiction works. Fiction is different; highlighting can happen anywhere. When I'm highlighting fiction, I'm usually noting recurring themes, but your teacher will probably guide you towards what you should be focusing on.
>
> Commenting in the margins should be used for any comments or notes you have on the reading. It is also called annotating. I use comments to state my opinion of the author's argument, argue against a point, agree with an issue, and connect what I am reading to

everything else I've learned about this topic. If you are renting or borrowing the book or article you are reading; you can also use sticky notes.

Asking questions is important. I usually also write these in the margins when something confuses me. The author will either answer this question later (yay), or I will have something to ask when the teacher calls for questions about the reading (double yay.) Either way, I'll write the answer under my question in the margins, so I always have it.

Summarizing key points helps you check your understanding of long passages and eases your studying later. Summarizing is the ability to pull out the main idea of passages like paragraphs and chapters, and I usually write my summarizations in the margins next to those passages. It helps me find information more quickly when I'm studying later on.

Overall, active reading strategies like these help you prepare for class, kickstarting your learning before class begins.

Lesson 8: Engage with the supplemental material. It helps broaden your understanding.

You should also read any supplemental material you have access to. Sometimes teachers will post articles or links on the classroom website without formally assigning them, or they'll say that a particular reading is optional. If you have time, you should read them anyway. Supplemental and optional materials give you a more well-rounded understanding of the required class material, especially when you actively read the supplementary readings.

Section 2: Making the Most of Class Time

Now you've got to class. Congratulations! It is the first big step on the way to academic success. Now that you're here let's talk about what you can do to maximize your classroom experience.

Attend class

This one sounds obvious, but it's true. The first step to permanently improving your grades is going to class, and class time can be maximized to give you the most advantages towards helping yourself later on.

Lesson 9: Be present during class, both physically and mentally.

You need to attend every single class meeting, especially if your grades are struggling. I know this may be hard work for some students, but the work put in directly corresponds to your success.

While you are in class, pay attention to what your teacher is saying. I have met a few teachers who just liked to hear themselves talk, but most teachers tell you things that you need to know. Class time is not a good time to catch up on your sleep, social media, or the other homework you haven't done yet. Devote your class time to that class's work, which includes things like actively listening to your teacher.

Lesson 10: Engage in active listening.

Active listening is a focused kind of listening that seeks to hear without focusing on being heard. It is usually used in private conversations, but the same skills can and should be applied to the classroom. When your teacher is speaking, check your body language. Sit up, look at your teacher, and nod when your teacher makes a point or a conclusion. While you should be taking notes (as we will discuss later on in this chapter), don't engage in any other kind of multi-tasking. Don't be on your phone, don't be passing notes to your friends, and don't be daydreaming. Work to keep yourself focused on the lesson, and only devote your attention there. With intentional focusing and proper body language to show that you are active in the listening process, you demonstrate your eagerness to learn, which subconsciously encourages your teacher to help you achieve your academic goals.

Classroom Hack: Sit in the T-Zone

It is a little-known classroom hack that increases your engagement with your teacher. In large classes, this helps your teacher remember who you are. In all size classes, sitting in the T-zone shows you are engaged in the lesson and eager to learn.

Lesson 11: Optimize the T-Zone.

The T-zone is a section of the classroom shaped like a 'T.' It includes the entire first row or two of seats (depending on the size of the classroom) and consists of the middle few seats all the way to the back of the room. Teachers subconsciously pay more attention to students in these areas of the room, so if you want better access to your teacher and the material, claim one of these seats for your own on your first day of class.

Now, some teachers use assigned seating, especially in middle school and going into high school. That's okay; don't fight the teacher about where you are sitting. You still have access to your teacher, but if you find yourself having trouble focusing from your assigned seat, talk to your teacher privately before or after class. If you ask politely to be placed in a different chair when assigned seating rotates again, most teachers are willing to accommodate your request and give you a better place to focus.

Ask Your Questions

I've known a lot of students who struggle with this. Asking questions, especially in front of the whole class, can be overwhelming for some people. That's okay. There's nothing wrong with this. All I ask is that you don't let your fear deprive you of your education.

Ask your teachers about anything you don't understand from the lecture, the readings, or notes. Your teacher doesn't know you have a question unless you ask, whether during class or privately afterward. If you are nervous, remember that the odds are if you have a question, someone else has the same one. On the flip side, pay attention when other students ask questions. You might find that their questions are also your questions.

Lesson 12: Ask specific, focused questions.

Try to keep your questions as straightforward as possible. Don't say that you just don't understand or ask about the subject in general. Here are a few examples of unfocused questions:

> 'What is the deal with circles?'
>
> 'I don't understand this class.'
>
> 'Who cares about Shakespeare anyway?'

These types of questions are too broad for your teacher to be able to help you, and they don't ask for the information and support you need. Try to narrow down your questions to a specific concept or lesson that you are confused about, however basic that idea may seem to you. Here are a few focused questions:

- 'I don't understand how the radius of a circle is connected to the circumference. Can you show me again?'
- 'How does this unit on cells relate to our last unit on atoms?'

- 'Are there other tools I can use to better understand Romeo and Juliet? I'm struggling with Shakespeare's use of language.'

Asking focused questions requires you to be introspective and discover what you need to ask questions about, but doing this allows you to focus your education on what you need to succeed.

Forge Study Buddy Alliances

Like just about anything in life, succeeding at school is easier if you have a support system. In class, I recommend the buddy system.

Lesson 13: Academic success is easier with a team of study buddies.

During the first couple of days of class, look around and identify one to three people who look like they could be good study buddies. They'll look a lot like you: open notebooks, textbook out, pen in hand. They'll look attentive and ready for class, even if they talk with other friends before class starts.

Once you have found a potential study buddy, introduce yourself. Become strong enough acquaintances that you can ask for a copy of their notes if you ever have to miss class or that you can invite them for a study session at the local library or coffee shop. We'll talk more later about how to maximize your study sessions with another student, but right now, while you are in class, work to build a safety net with an alliance of study buddies.

Section 3: Taking Notes

Note-taking is one of the make-it-or-break-it points for academic success. I have never known any student who could consistently achieve academic success who did not take notes in some way, shape, or form. Although the need to take notes in class is universally accepted, there are many different ways to do it. Part of this is because every person is unique. Part of this is because various subjects and classes require different note-taking strategies. However, you end up taking your notes, make sure you take them. It is one of the foundation stones of your academic success because the quality of your notes directly impacts the effectiveness of your study sessions and your test grades.

Handwritten Notes

I almost always recommend that students handwrite their notes whenever possible.

Lesson 14: Handwriting your notes increases brain engagement.

Although I have known people who were successful with typed notes, writing by hand activates more of your brain. The more brain engagement you have, the greater your memory retention. While this does not replace purposeful studying, it does give you a head start because your brain has already worked through this material once. Especially when someone is struggling in a class, one of my first recommendations is for them to handwrite their notes.

Avoid the Blob Method

There is only one note-taking method that I don't recommend because it rarely works: I call it the blob method. It is when the notes resemble one extremely long, stream-of-consciousness paragraph; it usually occurs when the student is trying to copy down every word the teacher says.

Lesson 15: The blob method is ineffective at best.

When Amanda came in for help with her algebra class, she was nearly hysterical because she was overwhelmed and didn't know how she would salvage her grade. As she showed me her notes, she mentioned that there was so much information that she would never be able to remember it all. Her notes looked like a blob of information; she had to read every single word of every single page to find what she was looking for when she studied. It was no wonder she was overwhelmed. Her notes were not structured in a helpful way, which made her studying more difficult later on.

We were able to save her grade because we changed how she took notes. She began using an outline organizational method, which, along with enhancing her other study skills, helped her pass the class.

Organizing Your Notes

There are many different ways to effectively organize your notes because every subject is diverse, and every student is different. The most important part of taking organized notes is the actual doing of it. The following organizational methods are what I have found to be effective in my years as a student and as a tutor; they are by no means all-inclusive. I encourage you to try them out and modify them as you need to. At the end of the day, your notes should be uniquely designed to aid you in your academic ventures.

Lesson 16: Outlining

It is the primary way I take notes, and I have found it effective with most of the students I have tutored. Start by writing the key term or main idea on the far left of your paper. Underneath that main idea, write all the pertinent information, and separate each concept with indented bullet points. You can indent as far as you need to organize all the information effectively during the lesson. As you are taking your notes, do not try to write in complete sentences, and do not try to copy your teacher verbatim unless your teacher tells you to write down a sentence or two exactly. Trying to write in complete sentences slows you down, which means you will probably miss important information. The outlining method means you can still see all the connections without all the connection words, making your notes quicker to take and more effective to use. Here's an example to base your outlining notes on.

<u>Example of good outline notes</u>

- One term = one bullet point
    - Indenting under means this is related to the above.
    - Multiple ideas not good for one bullet point
        - Too confusing later
- New concept = new bullet point
    - No complete sentences
        - Too long to write
    - Write important words and ideas
        - Symbols = effective
        - Abbreviations
            - & (and)
            - w/ (with)
            - b/c (because)
            - e.g. (for example)
            - i.e. (in other words)
        - Make up personal abbreviations.
            - Good for common, technical words
            - Unique to you and/or the class

Lesson 17: Highlighting

If your teacher talks slowly enough, highlight key terms and ideas as your teacher emphasizes them. Highlighting helps you immediately pick out the important information while studying: the only trick is making sure that you don't highlight everything. Highlighting everything produces the same effect in your brain as highlighting nothing: you cannot easily tell what is and is not essential.

Lesson 18: Color Coding

Color is also a great tool to help your brain focus on key concepts you want to remember. It helps your brain connect concepts together based upon color. If your teacher talks slowly enough, you can write in different colored pens to separate critical concepts, supporting ideas, and examples. You can also underline in colored pens or pencils.

If your teacher does not talk slowly enough for either of these note-taking strategies, don't worry. The best part of this strategy is that it can be done later as part of your study sessions. Re-reading your notes to highlight the key concepts or color code allows you to interact with the material once again, enhancing your ability to remember it.

Lesson 19: Writing in the Book

I have had classes where the teacher does not teach traditionally. Instead of discussing theories or key ideas that can be noted in a traditional note-taking manner, I've had teachers who taught from examples in the class book. These classes tend to be literature classes, such as English, or example-based courses, such as math.

Taking notes on a specific math problem or piece of literature is difficult to do in a notebook, although it can be done. For the literature, I recommend that students write directly in the book much like they would if they were actively reading. It is also called annotating. As your teacher discusses the piece of literature (whether it is a poem, a work of fiction, an essay, etc.), underline the key sections and write down the comments your teacher is making. It will help you learn the process for approaching the genre of literature you are learning and teaching you the intricacy of that specific work. For math, copy down the problem as your teacher shows you how to do it, but don't just write down the numbers. Next to each step, jot a short note explaining what each step is or does for the problem, such as 'combine like terms' or 'check answers for extraneous solutions.' It will help you learn how to do these types of equations and will help you remember when you are studying later on.

Chapter Review

- Get a planner to organize yourself.
- Sit in the T-Zone to make the most of class time.
- Use active reading and active listening to get the most out of your education.

- Ask your teacher all your questions.
- Find some study buddies. Education is not meant to happen in isolation.
- Handwrite your notes in an organized manner.

Chapter 3: Study Skills for Every Student

Here's where the rubber meets the road. To do well in classes, you have to learn the material. To do that, you need a study regimen. This chapter focuses on everything you need to know to establish and sustain a healthy and effective study regimen. So, grab a snack and your favorite beverage; we've got some studying to do.

Section 1: Location

You need to pick a good location for your study sessions. I recommend having no more than three distinct places where you typically do your schoolwork. I used to recommend having one place, but having three separate and distinct locations allows you some flexibility. My three locations were my kitchen table, a table at the back of the library, and my favorite coffee shop. I've had students who find they work best on their couch; others utilize an empty classroom. There are few wrong locations, but it's crucial you choose two or three as your primary studying places.

Consistency is Good for Memory

I emphasize having a few key locations because consistency is good for memory.

Lesson 20: Be consistent

Studying is all about learning the material so you can remember it. The human brain uses similarities to connect different experiences and information together. The more similar or consistent, the easier it is for your brain to find and retain the memory. It is why certain smells can make you nostalgic, or specific tastes can make you feel sick and uneasy. Your brain has recognized something familiar, pulled up a memory, and set your expectations for what you are experiencing now.

As a student, you can use this to your advantage by having a dedicated location to study. The habit of going to the same place with the same intention sets you up for success. Your brain will recognize that this is a time to study, and you will find it easier to focus and remember the material. The more consistent you can be, the better.

What a Good Location Has

There is an almost endless variety of locations you can choose to be your designated studying location, but here are some key aspects to look for as you decide.

Lesson 21: Good locations have all necessary supplies.

Your location needs to have access to everything you need. It ranges from research materials and whiteboards to a working bathroom and access to clean water. What you need will depend upon what you are doing and how you are studying. For example, the library was one of my designated study locations because I had access to my research materials while writing papers and whiteboards while studying for tests. Make sure your prospective location has everything you need to be successful.

Lesson 22: Good locations have the necessary atmosphere.

Your location should have an atmosphere that helps you focus. Some students need total silence to be able to concentrate; others need background noise. Some students study well with friends; others need to be alone. Find out what kind of atmosphere you need to study well, and make sure your prospective location can accommodate. You might find that you need different atmospheres for different tasks. For example, I wrote my essays best at my favorite coffee shop because there was enough noise to help me focus; however, I studied best in the silence of my own home or the back of the library. Everyone is different, so don't be afraid to discover what works for you and pick a location that best suits you and your study habits.

Lesson 23: Good locations are easily accessible.

Pick a study location that is easily accessible during your study times. If your site is only available once a week or you must drive a long distance to get to it, I advise that you pick a different place. Otherwise, you may start feeling discouraged about studying because your study location is difficult to get to. Your study locations should be easily accessible, which means that you will spend more time studying and less time worrying about your site.

Section 2: Time Management

Another big part of building a healthy study habit is proper time management. Staring blankly at your textbook for an hour is a waste of time, as is taking an hour to figure out what you want to focus on today. So, this section is focused on teaching you how to effectively manage your time during your study sessions, allowing you to be more efficient and productive at studying.

Use Your Planner

Pull out that planner that you set up back in Chapter 1. You should have already written in your class schedule, work schedule, and other appointments and meetings, so now we will focus on the blank spaces in your week.

Lesson 24: Plan your study times.

Using a highlighter or a colored pen, mark out blocks of time that you will dedicate to your study habits. I strongly recommend working on your schoolwork every day, but I also understand that is not possible for some students, especially if you are working while you are in school. At the minimum, you should be studying five days a week.

Set aside several hours of studying time in your planner for each session. Of course, every student is different, but I have found that many students can't focus for more than 2-3 hours without a long break. This long break could be eating dinner or having a coffee date with a friend so that you could schedule multiple study sessions in a day. I frequently did this on weekends and planned one study session per night on weekdays.

Lesson 25: Set study goals for yourself.

Once you have planned when you are going to study, set some goals for your study session. If you know what you will work on before you sit down to work, you will be more successful. These goals do not have to be elaborate, although they should be specific. Here are a few examples:

- I will finish my research for my history paper today and write a rough outline.
- I will do my Chapter 6, Unit 3 math homework, which is due Wednesday.
- I will review my vocabulary flashcards for my upcoming chemistry test for 30 minutes.

By setting these goals, you will give yourself something to work towards during each study session. As you start, write these goals in your planner, and check them off when you complete each one. It will give you a sense of accomplishment, encouraging you to keep going.

Cramming is Bad for You

As you plan your study sessions, be careful not to fall into the trap of cramming for tests. Cramming is when a student tries to learn all the material the night before the test. It may or may not include an all-nighter, which is when the student stays awake all night to cram.

Lesson 26: Cramming works against your brain's natural tendencies.

Cramming is actually not effective because it works against the natural tendencies of your brain. The human brain learns through repeating concepts and ideas, constructing relationships, and recognizing patterns. It takes time, and cramming does not allow you the time you need to understand the material. Trying to force everything into your short-term memory only increases your stress, further decreasing your brain's ability to recall accurately the material on your test the next day. Therefore, don't plan to do all of your studying the night before the test; certainly, don't plan all-nighters.

Lesson 27: Studying is like a marathon: slow and steady.

Instead of cramming, I recommend that my students begin studying approximately two weeks before the test is scheduled. I recommend reviewing for about 30 minutes a night, although you can increase that time if you need to. On the night before, though, I tell my students to review the material one last time and then go to bed. At this point, you already know the material, so attempting one last panicked study session isn't going to help you. Getting a good night's sleep will help you more. Sleep refreshes your brain, and if you review your notes right before you go to bed, your brain will process your notes as you sleep. Instead of cramming, the best preparation you can give yourself for an upcoming test is a dedicated study routine and a good night's sleep the night before.

Stick to Your Schedule

It is honestly the most challenging part about building and maintaining a study habit. Once you have planned your study schedule for the week in your planner, you should actually do it. I know that sounds obvious, but I also understand that this is the part that most students struggle with.

Lesson 28: Studying takes grit.

My advice is to build your study habit into your routine. I had one student who studied after dinner every night. I had another student who used her mornings as her study time. It doesn't matter when you review as much as it matters that you review regularly.

If you find you are struggling to focus, try to structure your study session with purposeful breaks. To start, work for 20 minutes and take a 10-minute break. Make sure you set a timer; otherwise, your break might grow uncontrollably. It is called the Pomodoro Method, and it comes in many variations. The short spurts of focused attention help you progress towards your goals, and the short breaks allow your brain to rest and prepare for the next spurt of focused attention.

Section 3: Study Techniques

Now that you have chosen a location and have figured out your study schedule, you can turn your attention to how you will study. There are hundreds of different studying techniques, but I will teach you the nine most efficient and effective study techniques I have found in my years as a student and a tutor.

The most important thing to remember is these studying techniques are not the only techniques you can use. Every student has different strengths, and every subject requires a different studying approach. Shape your study time for each subject to match your strengths. With a bit of introspection and experimentation, you will find the study techniques that work best for you. This list is here to get you started.

Lesson 29: Reading Your Notes

Reading your notes is one of the most fundamental study techniques. Regardless of whichever other study techniques you use, you will need to read your notes at some point. I suggest reading them often, especially the evening after your class. While you are reading them, try to focus on what you are reading. I sometimes struggled to focus, especially after a long day, so I would read my notes out loud to myself. The act of saying the words, hearing myself say them, and seeing them on the page helps increase memory retention, so try reading your notes out loud.

Also, don't be afraid to make notes on your notes. I tutored several students who highlighted and color-coded their notes after the lesson because it helped them identify important information and see connections more clearly. Other students added additional details in the margins, so they could find them when they needed them. Make your notes your own personal study guide and use your reading time to interact with them meaningfully.

Lesson 30: Flashcards

Flashcards are great for helping you memorize key terms, dates, and people. To make flashcards, I usually recommend a pile of blank index cards, although you can also use a folded sheet of paper. On one side of the index card, write the term, date, or person you need to memorize. On the other side of the index card, write down the information you need to know about that term, date, or person. Flashcards work best if you have small amounts of information, such as a definition or the name of a particular event. Putting too much information on a flashcard can be frustrating, which hampers your study time.

To use flashcards effectively, draw the first card from the pile and look at the term, date, or person. Without looking at the other side, try to remember the information. I usually recommend saying it out loud, even if so quietly that only you can hear. Once you have tried to remember the information, flip the card over and check yourself. If you have remembered correctly, place the flashcard into a completed pile. If you have not memorized accurately, put the flashcard into a stack to try again. Once you have gone through each flashcard once, go through the flashcards you need to try again. As you remember these cards correctly, place them into your completed pile. Use your time with your flashcards to memorize the material and connect the relevant information together. If you put in the work, flashcards will help you to learn the material.

Lesson 31: Mnemonic Devices

Mnemonic devices are memorization tools that can help you remember the order or relationship of information. These are usually words, phrases, or acronyms, and while there are some standard mnemonic devices that you can use, you can also create your own mnemonic device to suit your material and interests.

An example of a standard mnemonic device is used for the mathematical order of operations: Please Excuse My Dear Aunt Sally. Each word stands for a different mathematical operation: parenthesis, exponents, multiplication, division, addition, subtraction. This mnemonic device helps students remember the correct order of operations in an engaging way. You can create any type of mnemonic device you like for your information, so use this study skill to get creative with your study time. As you work with it, you will remember the information better because you took the time to learn creatively.

Lesson 32: Memorization

There are other memorization skills techniques other than flashcards and mnemonic devices. Memorization is all about repeating something until it is fixed into your long-term memory. It takes time, but the more you expose yourself to the information, the better your memory of it will be. There are different types of interactions, and they revolve around the senses of hearing, vision, and touch. You only remember 5% of what you hear and 10% of what you read if you do nothing else to supplement your learning. Incorporate as many sensory elements as possible into your study session:

- Write your notes by hand while reading them aloud to yourself.
- Practice repeatedly with different colors.
- Interact with other people about the class material.
- Get creative with how you memorize your material to find a combination of memorization techniques that work for you.

If flashcards or mnemonic devices do not work well with the information you are working on memorizing, you can write it out multiple times, preferably over multiple days. Say it aloud as you write and write in a red pen. Red naturally catches our memories more, so writing in red helps your brain remember the material better. Then, you can read over what you've written much like you would read over your notes.

Lesson 33: Concept Maps

Concept maps and diagrams can be fun to make, and they work well with interconnected material. I've used concept maps for science, history, and English classes. I usually recommend using a whiteboard if you have access to one (many libraries have whiteboards available for students), but you can also use a piece of paper. The most important part, to me, is having access to colors. I use different colors for different ideas and concepts, and I draw them out to visually see the relationships between them. This study skill helped me understand timelines better because I can see how one event influenced the next, and this study skill helped my students learn the cyclical patterns in science because they can draw the whole thing out.

There is no set form for a concept map. Each diagram should be drawn in a way that best showcases the material to you, so every time you draw a concept map, it might look different than any you've drawn before. That's normal. All I recommend is that you use colors and that if you work on a whiteboard, take a picture when you're done. It will allow you to reference your concept map later in your study session, making it useful to you in the future.

Lesson 34: Practice Problems

For more process-based classes, like math classes, I recommend working practice problems. While you can memorize the recommended process for a particular kind of problem or the rules associated with a certain function, it's hard to truly learn the process until you have done it many times. It is why I recommend practice problems to all of my students, regardless of what specific class they are taking.

Luckily, practice problems are easy to find. You can always work on the problems in your textbook that your teacher did not assign as homework, and the answers may be in the back, so you can check yourself as you work. If you don't have a textbook, you can search the Internet for practice problems. Type in the type of problems you are doing into your favorite search engine, and you will find many practice problems and examples to help you learn the process. Once you have a handle on what you are learning, you can even create your practice problems to solve. While you won't have an answer to check, you will find that creativity helps you solidify your understanding of your learning process.

Lesson 35: Creating Study Guides

Although you should already be studying and have a good grasp of the material, you can make a study guide to focus your remaining studying sessions as you get closer to the test. To make a study guide, you will need to anticipate what your teacher may put on the exam. Look over your notes and readings again for main ideas, key concepts, and important information. These are what teachers usually test over, so these should be your chief focus.

Once you have identified the critical information, create some questions about this information. Anticipate what your teacher may ask about this information and how your teacher will phrase these questions. Don't worry about making your questions exactly like your teachers. This study guide is meant to help you anticipate what will be on the test so that you can better prepare for it. Once you have created some questions, answer them. Use this study skill to help you focus on the material in the last few days before the test; your critical thinking and interactions with the material will help finish your preparations for the upcoming test.

Lesson 36: Study Groups

As you get closer to the test, you may also wish to form a study group. If you have made study buddy alliances, this will be easy: ask your study buddies when they are available to meet and study together. If you have not made study buddy alliances yet, this is the time to do so. Identify a couple of people in your class who are also good students and ask if they are willing to meet for a study session. I recommend meeting your study group in a public space, such as a library or a coffee shop.

Study groups allow you to interact with the material more organically and naturally. You can ask each other questions, clarify misunderstandings, and quiz each other for the upcoming test. It encourages memorization, but study groups can quickly become unproductive if you are not careful. To prevent your study session from becoming more about socializing than studying, keep the conversation focused on the material. It will be easier if you build in breaks. For example, for every 25 minutes of reviewing, your group can relax and socialize for 5 minutes. Just make sure you set a timer to keep the group on track.

Lesson 37: Teach Someone Else

Once you have a strong understanding of the material, test yourself by teaching the material to someone else. It can be anybody—your study buddy, your best friend, your pet, etc. Present the material in an ordered manner, acting as though the person you are teaching does not know the material. As you are teaching, encourage your student to ask questions. If you don't know the answer, that's probably something you need to study again. One of the best ways to truly learn something is to teach it because you interact with information differently when you are teaching versus learning. If you can teach the material successfully, you know it.

Chapter Review

- Keep your study sessions consistent with both your time and your location.
- Use your planner to plan out study goals and effective study sessions.
- Don't cram the night before your test.
- Structure breaks into your study sessions.
- Effective memorization is all about repetition.
- Effective studying utilizes as many senses as possible to increase learning.

Chapter 4: Writing Papers for the Classroom

Good grades usually come from a compilation of your work throughout the entire class. One of the more overlooked parts of a good grade is well-written papers. Papers are generally a substantial portion of your grade, so it's important to write good ones if you want to improve your grades sustainably. In my years as a tutor, I have met many students who have never learned how to write a paper well, so this next section focuses on doing that. With a little intentionality and practice, you will successfully write papers for your classes and improve your grades.

Section 1: Doing Research

There are certain types of papers and essays (such as the personal narrative essay or response papers) that do not require outside research; however, almost every big paper (such as a research paper) requires outside research. Your teacher will generally tell you if the report involves research or not. When in doubt, it's best to stay on the safe side: ask your teacher for clarification and prepare yourself to do some research.

Research may sound intimidating, especially if you haven't done it before. At its foundation, research is the act of systematically investigating a topic to increase your knowledge and understanding of it. You do research to learn what the experts on this topic think about it. If your research is done well, you will become a little expert on this topic. In the current age, there are three main ways to do research that are available to all students: books, articles, and the Internet.

Researching with Books

Personally, I love researching with books. Books are stable and make me feel as though I am making progress in my research. Of course, researching with books comes with its struggles. There is no way to search a physical text for key terms automatically. Books can be rather long, with a lot of information you aren't researching. Don't let the physicality of books overwhelm you, though. Once you know how to navigate a book, you may find book research to be as much fun as I see it.

Lesson 38: Researching with books

As you begin your research, pull books that seem to relate to your subject of study. Grab more than you think you're going to need; you will probably end up discarding some of these books before you finish your research. Once you have your books, read through the table of contents and the index, located at the front and back of the book, respectively. If your topic is not listed there, you can safely discard the book from your research pile.

Lesson 39: Skimming

Now you have a stack of books that contain some reference to your topic. Beginning with the first book, skim the sections of the book that discuss your point. You do not have to read the whole book. Instead, scan the relevant sections. To effectively skim longer sections (such as entire chapters), read the first one or two paragraphs fully. Then read each subsequent paragraph's first and last sentence until you reach the last one or two paragraphs. Read these final paragraphs fully as well. It will significantly reduce your reading time without substantially decreasing your general comprehension. Academic writers tend to put the main idea of the paragraph in the first or last sentence of body paragraphs (which is anything that isn't an introduction or a conclusion), so you can gain a basic understanding of each paragraph by just reading these two sentences. If, as you are skimming, you find this book does not discuss the information you want to write about, discard the book from your research pile. This process will help you gain a basic understanding of your subject while also narrowing down what exactly you want to write about and narrowing down how many sources you must read.

Lesson 40: Note the relevant information.

Now that you have narrowed down your sources, read through those relevant sections again. Note any quotations or facts you might want to use in your paper. I have done this with sticky notes. I have also typed the quotes into my computer with appropriate citation information. This part of the research will take the most time, but it gives you the information you need to write your paper successfully. Read carefully but selectively, using each paragraph's first and last sentence to guide you to the most relevant information for your research paper.

Researching with Articles

Articles are another popular way to do research. While some people still use literary magazines and journals to find their articles (to do this, follow the same steps you used to use books for research), many students now use electronic databases to find articles. Most schools have them, but if you have questions or concerns about accessing your school's electronic database, ask your librarian. Librarians are experts on using databases and can even help you find books and articles for your research paper.

Lesson 41: Finding articles on a database

Databases help you find articles with the use of a search engine. To begin, type in your subject using broad terms. It should pull up hundreds of articles, but don't worry. You don't have to read them all. Instead, start narrowing down your search. You can limit your search by publication date, by language, and by author. You can also narrow your search by narrowing your search terms, which will pull up fewer and fewer articles.

Lesson 42: Use the abstracts to narrow your search.

Once you have a manageable number of articles (I usually like to have around 20), start reading the titles and summaries. These summaries are usually about a paragraph long and are called abstracts. Good abstracts provide an overview of what the article argues and any conclusions the article draws. Suppose the abstract does not discuss your topic or the information you want to discuss in your paper; discard the report. It will help you to narrow the articles down further.

Lesson 43: Note all relevant information.

Now that you have narrowed the articles to only a few, you can read the articles. I suggest skimming at first to make sure the article discusses what the abstract says it discusses. Once you are certain, you can read the article fully—mark specific quotations and facts you might want to use in your paper. I usually printed my articles to increase my ability to actively read, highlighting and annotating my articles. You can also type the relevant quotations into your computer with the appropriate citation information.

Researching Online

The Internet is the most popular information tool we have today. You can find just about anything you want or need on the Internet, so it is a valuable research tool. However, researching on the Internet can be difficult because of the sheer volume of information. If you decide to use the Internet, you will need to know how to use this tool to efficiently and effectively find the sources and information you need to write your paper.

Lesson 44: Internet research tools

You can use tools to narrow your searches in your favorite search engine, and most of them pertain to how you type your search terms into your favorite search engine. Using these tools helps narrow your search, sometimes dramatically, allowing you to have quicker access to the information you need.

If your search term is more than one word—and you need your search term to appear all together—start by putting quotation marks around it. For example, if you are researching homemade volcanos using baking soda and vinegar, you could type in "baking soda." It tells the search engine only to pull up sources that discuss baking soda, not just baking or just soda.

If you have multiple search terms that work together, you can combine them with an AND. For example, your research on homemade volcanos might use the search term "baking soda" AND vinegar. It tells the search engine only to pull up sources that discuss baking soda and vinegar together.

If you have a search term you don't want to be included in your search, you can exclude it with a NOT. For example, you might use this in your research on homemade volcanos like this: "baking soda" AND vinegar NOT cleaning. It tells the search engine to exclude any source that contains the word 'cleaning.'

Lesson 45: Vary your search terms.

As you continue to hunt for sources, you should also change your search terms. It will allow the search engine to pull in new sources you haven't seen yet. For example, you could change your search terms after you have exhausted your search for "baking soda" AND vinegar NOT cleaning. You could switch to "homemade volcano" AND "baking soda." It will pull up some new sources (and many of the old sources), allowing you to continue your research on the Internet.

Lesson 46: Google Scholar

While you can use any search engine to find sources for your research paper, Google Scholar is specifically designed for students doing research. This search engine only pulls up articles, news stories, reports, and other works used in the academic setting. If you are concerned about finding literary sources, I suggest using Google Scholar as your search engine of choice.

Section 2: Outlining and Creating a Thesis

Now that you have finished your research, you are ready to start writing your paper. While I have met a few students who can jump straight into drafting, I have found that more students are successful if they plan out their essay before they write it. It is called outlining, and it's the skeleton of your paper. The first and most crucial part of your outline is your thesis, so it's the first thing you should write down and the thing your whole essay is focused on. By taking the time now to plan out your essay, you will save yourself time and frustration later because your paper will be less likely to swerve off-topic if you know where you are aiming and how you are getting there.

What is a Thesis?

Zach told me that one of the areas he struggled with was writing essays. He didn't understand how to focus everything he had learned into a single paper, and he didn't know how to structure it. As a result, papers usually gave him anxiety, and he would procrastinate on them until it was almost too late for him to finish them.

Lesson 47: How to write a thesis

The first part of writing a good paper is deciding what your main argument is going to be. Every essay has one main point it argues, so first, you need to figure out what you want your paper to say. It is called a thesis.

Your thesis should be specific and arguable, which means that someone could reasonably argue the opposite of your view. It doesn't make your hypothesis wrong; on the contrary, having an argumentative thesis will strengthen your paper.

Lesson 48: Examples of weak theses

Here are a few examples of weak theses:

- William Shakespeare wrote a lot of plays during his life.
- The Constitution was not the first governmental document for the United States, and that still affects the United States today.
- This paper is going to talk about how Isaac Newton invented calculus and what he did with it.

The first example thesis is not an argument; it's a fact. For you to build your paper around your view, you need to be arguing something.

The second example thesis is too broad. Your hypothesis should be specific and as concrete as possible. Your reader should be able to read your thesis and know exactly which points you will be presenting in your paper.

The third example thesis is also not an argument. When you write your thesis, you don't need to use words like "this paper will discuss" or "I will argue." It's your thesis; of course, it is what you are arguing and what your paper will discuss. Simply write down whatever your main point is. Remember, just because we are talking about how a thesis is an argument does not mean that factual papers can't have a theory (quite the contrary: see revised example thesis 2). Your hypothesis can and often is an argument that someone has argued before. You are just presenting it in your way.

Lesson 49: Examples of strong theses

Here are a few examples of specific and argumentative theses:

- William Shakespeare's Hamlet changed the development of theatre in Elizabethan England by presenting an introspective main character.
- The Articles of Confederation directly influenced the writing of the United States Constitution by demonstrating the dangers of a decentralized government and a lack of federal taxation.
- Although Isaac Newton invented calculus accidentally, he then used it to revolutionize the scientific community of his day by demonstrating how calculus helps explain the observed movement of the stars.

These revised theses are all specific, argumentative, and give the main point of the paper. Now that we know what the theory of our essay is, we can start the outlining process.

How to Create an Outline

Once Zach was confident with writing theses, we moved on to writing a whole outline. It was a little overwhelming for him when he started, but once he realized that an outline is structured to support his thesis, he found it easier.

Essays do not have a definitive structure; instead, they are often uniquely structured in response to the thesis. Each paragraph has a point that it proves or a piece of evidence it defends that all support the paper's main thesis. If this is your first essay, though, that can be a little overwhelming, so I will teach you the structure for a five-paragraph essay. It will give you the foundation you need to outline other reports as you grow as a writer.

Lesson 50: The Five-Paragraph Essay

Here is the structure of a five-paragraph essay. From this structure, you can learn how to write papers and expand your writing skills.

Five-Paragraph Essay Structure:

- Introduction (thesis as your last sentence)
- Body Paragraphs (x3)
  - Topic Sentence
  - Evidence
  - Analysis

Evaluation

Conclusion

As you are outlining, write down your thesis statement under the introduction. Write what each of your three paragraphs will discuss, and make sure each of these paragraphs supports your overall thesis. I also usually recommend that students note what evidence they will use in each section because the evidence is gleaned from research. Of course, you can make your outline as detailed as you like, but this is what I usually recommend for students first learning how to outline and write papers.

As you are writing, the introduction should be a general overview of your paper. Start with an attention-grabber about your topic. It can be an interesting statistic, a comment upon recent discoveries concerning your subject, or an intriguing and relevant fact. Then, discuss what your paper will cover, and end the introduction with your thesis statement. Your introduction should be three to four sentences, especially if you are still practicing essay writing.

Each of the body paragraphs should be about a different topic that supports your overall thesis. Start each body paragraph with the topic sentence for that paragraph. Then, present a piece of evidence. This is a quotation, paraphrase, or summary from your research. Once you have presented and correctly cited your evidence, analyze it. Explain how your evidence supports your paragraph's topic sentence. Then, evaluate the evidence and your analysis. Explain why your evidence and analysis support your overall thesis. Repeat this process for each of the paragraphs and each piece of evidence you want to present.

The conclusion should start with your thesis statement. Then review what your paper covered by briefly discussing your three body paragraphs. It should take no more than two sentences, especially for three body paragraphs. Finally, conclude with a statement of reflection concerning how your paper connects or influences the broader world.

As you grow as a writer, you will find yourself branching away from this structure, especially in your body paragraphs. You will find that your evidence begins to intermingle with your analysis and your evaluation. It is normal; it's called weaving. Weaving is an academic writing technique where you weave your evidence with your analysis. It makes for stronger argumentation and a more robust paper because your words intermingle with experts' words. If this is your first paper, however, don't worry about weaving. The more you practice and the more you read, the better your writing skills will become. Practice with the five-paragraph essay and watch your writing skills grow.

Now Write!

Now that you have finished planning your essay, you need to write it.

Lesson 51: Drafting

Plan several study sessions to work on drafting your essay and push to finish it. The main thing to remember is that this is a draft, so it doesn't have to be perfect. Drafting is getting all your words and ideas onto paper; they don't need to be eloquent or grammatically flawless. You will fix that once you have finished the drafting process. To write a good first draft, all you should focus on is writing the rough draft down, so write.

Section 3: Revising versus Editing

Once you have finished drafting your essay, you can begin the revising and editing process. These are separate from the drafting process. Drafting is when you write all your thoughts, ideas, and evidence down, following your outline closely to maintain organization. Revising and editing are when you polish the paper and make it sound solid and eloquent. Good reports are born during the drafting stage, but you discover them during revising and editing.

How to Revise

Revising is the act of reexamining your paper to make alterations or to make your writing more efficient. You may find yourself taking sentences out, adding sentences in, or rewriting sentences completely. It is all a normal part of the revision process. Revision is not correcting grammar and usage; that's the editing stage.

Lesson 52: Making Revisions

Everybody needs to make revisions to their first draft, and I recommend starting at the beginning. Read your paper out loud and mark any spots that sound weird or where you think your argument is not strong. I like to write myself notes in the margins of my first draft, so I remember why I marked that sentence or paragraph.

Now that you have identified the areas most in need of revision rework them. You may need to add a sentence or rewrite something. As I was helping Zach learn the revision process, we discovered he needed to rewrite an entire paragraph because it didn't argue what he wanted it to. It is a natural part of the revision process. He ended up writing that paragraph three times before he was satisfied with it, and because he took the time to revise it carefully, his paper was stronger and more eloquent.

You can also reach out to friends, classmates, and teachers to help you revise. A fresh set of eyes can often see mistakes and areas of improvement better than you can, so don't be afraid to ask someone you trust for revision advice.

How to Edit

Editing is the act of correcting the technical errors of your paper. It is where you look at your grammar usage and make sure your sentences are all constructed properly.

Lesson 53: Editing Your Paper

If you have a strong understanding of grammar, then you should read through your paper two or three times to correct all your grammatical errors. With a strong knowledge of grammar, you should be able to see and fix a variety of different errors that may appear during the drafting process.

If you are still developing a solid understanding of grammar, I recommend you read your paper multiple times, each time looking for a different grammatical concept you are working on. For instance, the first time you read, you could look for subject-verb agreement. The second time you read, you can look for correct comma usage.

If you find yourself reading without really seeing the words anymore—or you have read your paper multiple times already—then you can read your paper backward. Start at the last sentence and work your way to the beginning of your essay, one sentence at a time. It will help you find grammatical errors that you had otherwise missed.

As you are editing, don't be afraid to also reach out to others who have a strong understanding of grammar and usage. Ask a friend or a teacher to read your paper. Some schools even have Writing Centers or tutoring, and these places are staffed with people who are willing and able to help you with your writing. All you have to do is ask.

Basic Grammar Rules to Remember

English grammar can be daunting if you do not have a strong understanding of its basic rules. To help you gain confidence in your editing skills, I have listed some basic English grammar rules. This list is by no means exhaustive, but it should give you the foundation you need to grow and nourish your grammatical skills.

Lesson 54: Subject-verb Agreement

Every sentence should have a subject and a verb. A subject is who or what the sentence is about. A verb is what the subject is doing or what the subject is.

Subjects and verbs come in the first, second, and third person. They also come in singular and plural forms. Here is a chart outlining common subjects to help explain it.

First person singular: I	First person plural: We
Second person singular: You	Second person plural: You (all)
Third person singular: He, She, It	Third person plural: They

The form of the verb you use should agree in person and number with the subject you use.

Here are a few examples of subject-verb disagreement:

> It are rare.
>
> Sally grow hungry.
>
> I likes to run.

To fix this disagreement, we must match the subject to the correct form of the verb. Here are the corrected sentences.

> It is rare.
>
> Sally grows hungry.
>
> I like to run.

By ensuring subject-verb agreement, you decrease confusion in your paper, and you help your reader focus on your argument instead of on your subjects and verbs.

Lesson 55: Periods

Every sentence you write should have an end mark of some kind. There are three traditional end marks in English: the period, the question mark, and the exclamation point. Question marks are used to denote a question, and exclamation points are used to denote a statement of great emotional impact, usually excitement or frustration. In academic writing, though, you won't typically use the exclamation point at all unless you are writing a narrative essay. If so, you might use one in the entire narrative essay.

The most common end mark you will use is the period. Every sentence should end with a period (unless it ends with a question mark or an exclamation point), and every sentence should start with a capital letter. I know some of you may think this simple, but I include it here because I have read papers written by college students that do not follow this grammatical principle. As such, their reports were nearly impossible to understand. Help your reader follow your writing and your thoughts; finish your sentences with a period.

Lesson 56: Commas

Commas were one of the punctuation marks Zach really struggled with. Commas have many different roles to fulfill in sentence construction, and Zach hadn't ever been taught the rules. Personally, I understand and agree with him—there are a lot of comma rules. For your academic papers, these are the foundational rules you should follow and live by.

1. By itself, a comma cannot create a compound sentence. It is called a comma splice. Here is an example of a comma splice: It snowed all morning, then the sun came out.
   Both "it snowed all morning" and "then the sun came out" are independent clauses (this means they can stand on their own as complete sentences. They each have a subject and a verb, and they do not have any subordinating words

or phrases). You cannot properly join two clauses with only a comma.
To fix this comma splice, you can take one of these three corrective steps.

    a. You can use a conjunction. The sentence would look like this: It snowed all morning, but then the sun came out.
    b. You can write each clause as its own sentence. The sentences would look like this: It snowed all morning. Then the sun came out.
    c. You can replace the comma with a semicolon. The sentence would look like this: It snowed all morning; then the sun came out. Personally, until you have learned the rules of semicolons, I would advise against fixing your comma splices with semicolons. Just like commas, semicolons have their own grammatical conventions and regulations, so wait to use them until you know how. Almost all grammar books have a section on semicolons; I suggest you investigate.

2. When you join two independent clauses with a conjunction, put a comma before the conjunction. The conjunctions that always take commas are for, and, nor, but, or, yet, and so. You can use the mnemonic device FANBOYS to remember these coordinating conjunctions. Here is an example of this grammatical principle: My dog wanted to go for a walk, so my kid offered to go with her.

3. Put a comma after an introductory phrase. A phrase is not able to be a complete sentence on its own. It is missing either a subject, a verb or is dependent on another part of the sentence for full meaning. Dependent phrases usually contain subordinating language (such as unless, although, because, or despite), and when at the beginning of the sentence, they serve as an introduction to the sentence. This introductory phrase should have a comma after it to separate it from the rest of the sentence. Here is an example of an introductory phrase: While waiting for the doctor, I worked on my crossword puzzles.
4. Use commas when writing out a list. After every item on the list, except for the very last one, you should put a comma to separate the items.

Here is an example: I went to the store to buy milk, oranges, green beans, detergent, and chocolate.

Lesson 57: Homophones/homonyms

Homophones (or homonyms) are words that sound the same but are spelled differently. The three main homophones I teach my students are as follows.

To/Too/Two

To is a preposition that generally designates movement or indicates an infinitive verb.

Too is another way to say 'also.'

Two is the number 2.

You're/Your

You're is the contraction for *you are*.

Your is the second person possessive. It indicates that something belongs to you.

There/Their/They're

There is a designation of location.

Their is the third person possessive. It indicates that something belongs to them.

They're is the contraction for *they are*.

The Importance of Proofreading

Once you have finished outlining, drafting, revising, and editing, you may be tempted to say you're done, but there is one more step.

Lesson 58: How to Proofread

The last thing you need to do is read your paper one last time, preferably a day or two after you have finished revising and editing. Proofreading is the final check to make sure your paper is logical and argues your point. When you find an error, correct it. Let this last checkup smooth over any final creases or rough transitions, and then congratulate yourself. You just finished writing a good paper.

Section 4: Time Management

Writing a good paper requires more than having the right techniques; you also need to allow enough time to complete the process. You need more time than you may think to write well because the creation process takes time. Determination and practice help to streamline the process, but you still need a good deal of time to write an essay well.

What Not to Do

Over the years, I have helped many students develop healthy writing habits. When Zach first came to me, he told me about how he usually waited until the night before a paper was due to write it because he didn't know what to write about or how to start.

Lesson 59: Don't Procrastinate

That's the first unhealthy habit we worked though: procrastinating until the last minute does not help you. Procrastination usually relies upon panic or anxiety to get something done, which isn't healthy for you and doesn't produce good work. Instead of procrastinating, I suggest students plan specific times for specific parts of the writing process. I also suggest you start your writing process at least two weeks before the paper is due. As you grow as a writer, you will learn how much time you need for each section of the writing process and should adjust your time allocations accordingly.

Lesson 60: Research Strategically

Other students are overwhelmed by their research. I understand how research can be challenging to work through; there's so much information on almost any topic you choose to write a paper about that it can all be overwhelming. My advice is to be strategic. Choose reliable sources that will give you good information. Try to collect a sampling from the whole field, but also keep your number of sources at a manageable level. If your teacher does not give you a source minimum, then I suggest you have two more sources than the required number of pages for your paper. So, if your paper is supposed to be five pages long, strive for seven reliable sources. It should help you limit your stress about research and keep you from misallocating your time.

Lesson 61: You Can Write.

Other students are daunted by the writing process. They feel like they can't write, so they don't. These students always make my heart hurt because they do not believe in themselves. They don't know that, in its original language, 'essay' meant 'to try.' Essays do not have to be perfect. Your teacher does not have to agree with the argument of your paper. All I am asking when you write an essay is that you try. Try to explain why you believe what you believe. Try to argue logically. Try to persuade me to agree with you. Essays are all about showing your thought process and argumentation skills as you analyze the evidence. Don't allow the writing process to daunt you because essays are just about trying.

Use Your Planner

As you are preparing to write your essay, pull out your planner.

Lesson 62: Keep Using Your Planner to Manage Your Writing Process.

If you have been keeping up with your planner, you should be able to quickly see some available blocks of time in the next two weeks. Mark in time to work on your essay, beginning with research and ending with your final proofread. Stretch your work over two weeks. It allows you to work steadily without panicking. If this is your first essay, plan for 3-5 days of research. Then, prepare 3-4 days for drafting and then a rest day. Professional writers use rest days to clear their minds, which allows them to revise and edit with fresh eyes. Finally, use the last 4-7 days to revise and edit your essay. Of course, as you grow as a writer, you will morph this template to fit your writing needs. You may find you need 8 days of research to understand a topic fully. As you grow, you will build your own writing habit, including days and times for each part of the writing process. Write it down in your planner as you develop it to help you stay on track.

Stick to Your Schedule

Staying on track is the hardest part. It requires determination and self-discipline, which can be challenging at times.

Lesson 63: How to Help Yourself Stay on Track

If you find you are struggling to keep to the schedule in your planner, plan rewards into your writing process. Prizes can help you develop and maintain your determination. Still, they don't have to be big—I would purchase a hot chocolate from my favorite coffee shop when I finished my paper (and usually when I finished my research).

I also recommend focusing tools. For some people, music helps them to focus. Classical music has been particularly effective at assisting people in focusing because it does not have words; however, I also know students who focus best on hard rock or country. Fidget tools can also help, although I do not find them to be as effective when a student needs both of their hands to type. Chewing gum can also help, and gum has the benefit of being a fidget tool without monopolizing your hands. There are many different ways to focus and maintain determination, so all I suggest is that you find one that works for you and build it into your writing and academic habits.

Chapter Review

- Narrow down your research materials before you begin reading. Skimming is very helpful here.
- Write an argumentative thesis for your paper.
- Outline before you begin drafting.
- Revision focuses on examining your paper for efficiency and clarity of argument.
- Editing focuses on technical and grammatical accuracy.
- Don't procrastinate on your essay. Start at least two weeks before the due date.

Chapter 5: Acing Tests

Tests are, without a doubt, one of the biggest sources of anxiety for students. I work with many students who have great anxiety about taking tests. Amanda was one of those students; as she and I were prepping for an upcoming test, she told me about how she never seemed to be able to remember anything during an exam. She panicked, felt like she had forgotten everything, and did not perform to her usual standard. This sort of anxiety is common among students because the education system places a disproportionate emphasis on achievement. Thankfully, I have enjoyed helping many students overcome their fears about test-taking with tips and strategies that help you focus and demonstrate your long preparation. All you need to be successful is to be prepared.

Section 1: General Testing Tips

No matter what type of test you are taking or how seasoned you are at taking them, I have some general test-taking tips to improve your testing abilities. Some of these skills focus on taking care of yourself because self-care is essential to the success of all sorts and types, including academics. The rest of these skills focus on how to actually take a test with emphasis upon answering the questions well. Once you have these skills under your belt, you will be able to handle any type of test with confidence.

Take Care of Yourself

Taking care of yourself is one of the essential life skills I have ever taught my students. Many of my students come to me as Amanda did. She was so stressed about her grades that she wasn't sleeping much, was eating poorly and erratically, and had not seen her friends in weeks. Even though she was spending all her time studying, her test grades weren't improving because she wasn't taking care of herself.

Lesson 64: Your Self Care Affects Your Grades.

Taking tests well is as affected by how you take care of yourself before and during the test as by what you do on the test. So, the first thing you can do to improve your test scores is to take care of yourself. Strive to sleep for at least 8 hours a night, especially on the night before your test. If you have been studying properly along the way, staying up late will not help you learn the material better; it will actually decrease your memory retention because your brain will be sleep-deprived.

You should be eating good meals at regular intervals, and on the night before your test, you should especially certainly eat a good dinner. When you wake up if you can stand it, eat a good breakfast as well. The food will help kick start your brain and give it the necessary nutrients to perform well.

Breathe

Once you sit down to take your exam, take a second to evaluate how you are feeling. I know I was always a little nervous right before a test, and I've found that most of my students are also nervous before a test.

Lesson 65: Remember to Breathe.

If you feel butterflies in your stomach, take a deep breath. Let the oxygen flow up to your brain, which will also help it to perform better. Tell yourself that you have prepared for this exam, and then dive into the first question. You may just find that you know this material better than you think you do.

Lesson 66: Test Anxiety

Now, some of my students are more than a little nervous. They are downright anxious, and some of them have been diagnosed with test anxiety. They get to a test and panic often because they view a test as a measure of their self-worth. They are so anxious to perform well that they get in their own way. They second guess every answer, convince themselves they don't know how to proceed, and often run out of time. These students usually perform well on the homework and bomb the tests, which tells me that we are working through anxiety, not academic failure. While I am not a medical professional, I have found that the best way to help my students is to teach them skills to reduce panic.

Lesson 67: Dealing with Test Anxiety

The first thing we do is reframe how my students think of testing. Tests are not a measure of your self-worth; instead, tests are simply another worksheet. It is only another assignment; this one just happens to be timed.

I also encourage my student to breathe. If you are panicking, you probably aren't breathing deeply enough, and your brain needs the oxygen anyway. Another way to bring yourself back is, if you're allowed a water bottle, take a sip of water every time you hit a question that makes your anxiety spike. It pauses the anxiety and enables you to get ahead of it.

My students also write on their tests. They will fill the top and margins with notes to themselves, formulas they need to remember, and everything they know about challenging questions. Having it all on paper takes away some of the stress of remembering it during the test. All you have to do is write it down from memory the moment you receive your exam and refer back to it while you answer the questions.

I have had the joy of helping many of my students work through their anxiety. Each student needs a different tool kit, so I encourage you to use these suggestions and find what works for you. As you are working through it, remember that I am proud of you. You have already come so far just by trying to gain control over your anxiety. No one celebrates more than I do over an improved test score; when Amanda came in with a 73 instead of her usual 59, it was one of the happiest sessions we had. Take each test as it comes, work through your anxiety with a support system, and celebrate each slight improvement along the way.

Again, I am not a medical professional. I cannot diagnose anything, and I cannot treat anything. All I can do is offer advice gained from years of working with other students. If your anxiety about testing extends to other areas of your life, or you just feel like you need more support, please reach out to a therapist or a doctor. They will provide you with more individualized support and a treatment program, and I strongly recommend you allow them to help you.

What is the Question Actually Asking?

Once you sit down to the test and read the first question, take a moment to verify what the question is asking.

Lesson 68: Rephrase the Question

Some questions are simple; for example, 'What was the purpose of the Stamp Act?' is a simple question. Some questions are complicated, though, and these questions require you to identify what is being asked. An example of a more complex question is 'How did the Stamp Act and the Sugar Act impact the civil unrest leading up to the American Revolution?' This question asks you to describe the effects of these two acts on the American colonists; a way to rephrase the question would be 'How did the American colonists react to the Stamp Act and the Sugar Act?' To answer more complicated questions, first, identify the keywords of the question. Then, rephrase the question to yourself, so you know what the question is really asking. Once you understand the question, you will be able to answer it.

How to Answer Questions You Don't Know

Sometimes you come across a question you don't know the answer for.

Lesson 69: Answering Difficult Questions

When this happens, the first thing I want you to do is to start writing next to the question everything you do know about the question. It often helps to jog your memory. If the question is a multiple-choice question, eliminate the answers you know to be wrong.

If you still can't figure out how to answer the question, put a star next to it and move on to the next question. Don't let yourself spend the entire test on one question; instead, mark the questions you don't know and come back to them once you have finished answering all the other questions. Something else on the test may give you a hint or help you remember how to answer a difficult question.

Whatever you do, don't leave answers blank. If you run out of time, make an educated guess on the remaining questions. It is better to guess than to leave an answer blank because you are more likely to get the answer right if you guess than if you don't answer at all.

Section 2: Multiple Choice Tests

Multiple-choice tests are a popular form of testing. They involve a series of questions with answer choices, usually four. The purpose of this type of test is for you to select the correct answer from amongst the incorrect answers.

How to Approach Each Question

Each question deals with a different topic or concept from the unit.

Lesson 70: Multiple Choice Test Taking Tips

Read each question carefully. Underline or circle the key terms to make sure you understand what the question is asking. Before you look at the answer choices, try to formulate the answer in your head. Once you have an answer, look at the answer choices and pick the option that is closest to the correct answer.

Use the Answer Choices to Your Advantage

If you come to a multiple-choice question you don't know the answer to, look at the answer choices.

Lesson 70: Answers Choices Can Help You Pick an Answer.

Unless the instructions tell you otherwise, each question has only one correct answer, so start by eliminating the obviously wrong answers. It may limit your choices down to one possibility, and this single choice will be the answer.

If eliminating wrong answers does not remove all other options, look over the question again. See if one of the remaining options is more suitable or more accurate than the other one. Some multiple-choice tests have answer choices that are similar but not the same. One of them will always be more correct than the other, and you should choose the more accurate answer choice.

If reviewing the question again does not help, mark the question with a star and come back to it. As you continue through the test, you might find that another question can help you figure out the answer to this one.

Section 3: Essay Tests

Essay tests are often used to determine your ability to explain, analyze, and evaluate what you have learned. They ask you to answer a question with an essay, so there isn't a single right answer. To do well on an essay test, you must be able to explain the information and defend your point with what you have learned.

How to Approach the Question

Essay tests are usually timed, just like most other tests, so start by reading the question.

Lesson 71: Tips for How to Take an Essay Test

Underline the key terms to make sure you know what exactly the question is asking—there's nothing more frustrating than writing a whole essay on the wrong topic. Once you fully understand what the question asks, take 3-5 minutes to plan your essay. I suggest a brief outline on a blank section of the test. Write down your thesis, using as many of the key terms as possible and three main points. Each of these main points will be body paragraphs in your essay. As you get more experienced with timed essays, you may start adapting how many points you have in your timed essay, but as you are learning, strive for three body paragraphs.

Once you have planned your essay, immediately start writing it. Try to write as neatly and accurately as possible, but don't spend a lot of time worrying about it. Timed essays are inherently rough drafts; your teacher is not expecting a perfect or even polished essay. All you need to do is stick to your outline. Resist the urge to follow tangents to fill space; it is much more important that your essay be coherent and argue one point than for your essay to be long.

Once you have finished writing your timed essay, read over it again. Correct grammatical errors, and make sure your paper supports your thesis throughout the whole thing. Use this time to verify your essay is accurate, even if it's not perfect.

Section 4: Other Types of Tests

There are other types of tests other than the multiple-choice and the essay test. While sometimes these tests stand on their own, other times these types of questions can appear in different sections on one test. Don't let that throw you; instead, take a moment to read the instructions and situate yourself in each part before jumping in and answering the questions.

Matching Tests

The purpose of a matching test is to select which term goes with which description.

Lesson 72: Matching Test Tips

The number of terms and descriptions on your test can vary widely, but unless the instructions tell you otherwise, each description goes with only one term and vice versa. Therefore, you should approach matching tests similarly to how you approach multiple-choice tests. As you read through each term, try to remember the description for it. Find the description that best matches your answer, match the two together, and then cross the description off your list. It will help you to narrow down the potential definitions for any terms you don't remember.

Short Answer Tests

Short answer tests are like essay tests but shorter.

Lesson 73: Short Answer Testing Tips

Instead of a whole essay, a short answer test usually means you need to write 3-4 sentences to answer the question. Like an essay test, make sure you fully understand what the question asks before you answer it. Read over each answer once you are done to ensure you responded to the question completely and accurately. Including as many key terms as possible (usually borrowing from the question itself) can help you stay on topic and completely answer the question.

True-False Tests

True-false tests assess your ability to separate correct and incorrect information about the class material.

Lesson 74: Tips for True-False Tests

These tests are usually set up as a series of individual statements, some of which are true and some of which are false. Read each sentence carefully and determine if it is correct or incorrect. A statement is wrong or false if any part of the statement is false. For example, the sentence 'George Washington was the second president of the United States is incorrect, even though George Washington was a United States president. Mark all inaccurate statements as false and all correct statements as true. If you are unsure, mark the question with a star and come back to it after completing the other questions on the test. You might find you have a better recollection after finishing the other questions.

Chapter Review

- Practice good self-care as you prepare for a test.
- Remember to breathe.
- If you think you have test anxiety, visit your doctor.
- Make sure you actually answer the question.
- Don't spend too much time on any one question. If you are unsure, star the question

and come back to it after you have completed the rest of the test.

Chapter 6: Tackling Other Projects

In addition to writing essays and taking tests, your teacher may ask you to demonstrate your knowledge of the class material through a project. It may include giving a presentation or working on a group project. These kinds of projects present unique opportunities to you, but some of my tutoring students find special projects challenging. Therefore, this chapter will focus on overcoming the challenges of school projects to showcase your thorough understanding of the class material and further improve your grades.

Section 1: Crafting a Presentation

Class presentations are often a source of anxiety for my students. They don't know how to craft them, and they don't know how to give them. While the next section will focus on speaking well in public, this section focuses on preparing your presentation. If you craft your presentation effectively, you will increase your success rate and raise your confidence.

Purpose of a presentation

Much like writing an essay, you should always create a presentation with a purpose in mind. Your teacher will probably give you your purpose, and it may be over the same information you wrote your paper about. There are many different types of presentations you can choose from, depending upon your intended purpose.

Lesson 75: Informative Presentations

Informative presentations are meant to inform your audience about a particular topic, idea, or discovery. These types of presentations do not take a side on any issue; instead, they seek to inform or teach the audience about a particular topic. Teachers in the classroom often use informative presentations to teach their students the lessons.

Lesson 76: Argumentative Presentations

Argumentative presentations are meant to persuade your audience to accept your viewpoint on a topic or issue. These presentations are all about persuasion techniques, and they firmly take one side of a problem. Argumentative presentations typically demonstrate the benefits of their chosen side and the deficiencies of the opposing side to persuade an audience. Good argumentative presentations, though, are not rude or dismissive of opposing viewpoints. They seek to influence, and rudely dismissing opposition is not usually persuasive. Politicians often use argumentative presentations to persuade the people on a particular current issue.

Lesson 77: Academic Presentations

Academic presentations are a combination of informative presentations and argumentative presentations. It is closest to the essays you write.

There is some main point you are arguing (a thesis), but you are also presenting information (evidence and your interpretation of it) to support your argument. Academic presentations seek to inform their audience about a topic while also making an argument about it, much like your research papers. It will most likely be the type of presentation you give most often in the classroom when your teacher asks for a presentation.

Structure it like an essay

The best way to structure your presentation is to structure it like an essay. Essays follow the same logical pattern that a presentation should follow, so it's a good foundation you can work off of.

Lesson 78: Constructing Your Presentation

Start your presentation with an introduction. Start with an interesting fact or short story (this is called an attention-grabbing device) and then state the main point of your presentation. It is a little different from an essay; in a paper, you give your thesis as the last sentence in your introduction. In a presentation, your view should be as close to the beginning of your presentation as possible because your audience is more likely to hear your thesis if it is close to the opening.

After you have introduced your topic:

1. Go through each point much as you would in an essay.

2. Present your evidence, analyze it, and evaluate it.
3. Be clear about how each issue relates back to your central thesis to help your audience remember what you are presenting.

When you conclude, remind your audience once again what your thesis is. Then review your main points and end with a possible application of your theory and presentation to the larger world. It could be a call to action in some presentations, where you encourage the audience to do something.

How to Prepare Visuals

When most students prepare a visual aid for their presentation, they prepare a PowerPoint (or some variant thereof). Effectively crafting your visuals is as essential as preparing your presentation effectively because your visual aid will either detract or enhance your presentation.

Lesson 79: Avoid Overcrowding

The most crucial tip for setting up an effective PowerPoint is don't crowd your slides. A PowerPoint slide over-filled with words and pictures is distracting, and your audience will ignore what you are saying to read your slide. A crowded slide is also overwhelming. If you put too much information on the slide, your audience won't know what to focus on, leaving them unable to focus on your point.

The first thing you can do to avoid crowding your slides is limit your words. I usually strive for 3-5 bullet points per slide, with no more than 3-7 words per bullet point. Don't write in complete sentences. It dramatically increases your word count without increasing your effectiveness. Your PowerPoint should aid your presentation, but you shouldn't be reading off of it. It should give the main idea of each point and potentially any specific quotations or statistics you need to remember and present exactly.

The second thing you can do to avoid crowding your slides is to make your pictures strategic. Don't just put pictures onto your slide because they look pretty; images should enhance your point or provide a visual for a specific term or idea. Unless I have several words that require a visual, I limit myself to one picture per slide. Of course, if I have several terms that need visual representations, I put in the images I need, but the most I have put onto a single PowerPoint slide is three. Also, make sure you cite any picture you use somewhere in your PowerPoint. Plagiarism applies to images as well as words.

Lesson 80: Basic PowerPoint Etiquette

PowerPoints offer a wide variety of design opportunities, and I have seen many PowerPoints where students fully exercised their creativity. Some of those presentations were works of art; others were impossible to read.

To make sure your audience can fully appreciate your PowerPoint, start by picking good colors. In general, your words should be an opposite color from your background. For example, if you have a white backdrop, you should use black letters. If you have a navy background, you should use white letters. Try to stick to neutral colors (white, black, navy, etc.) that are gentle on the eyes. Your audience will not appreciate having to squint and strain to read your slide, so as you are creating, you should change its colors if you think something might be a little difficult to see.

Once you have picked a good color palette, increase your font size. Your slide should be easily readable from the back of the room, especially if anyone in your class has vision complications. At the minimum, your font should be sized 26, although the larger your font is, the easier it is to read.

Now that your slides are beautiful, you might be tempted to get creative with your transitions. Some of the transitions are impressive, and I enjoy scrolling through them. Although you may be tempted to use all of your favorites, you should keep your transitions consistent throughout the presentation. Multiple elaborate shifts are also distracting to your audience. It can detract from the information you are presenting, so be constant with your transitions. I also usually suggest a simple transition or transition related to your presentation topic to further enhance your presentation without distracting your audience.

Section 2: Public Speaking

I can still remember the panicked look on Zach's face when he told me his teacher had assigned class presentations. He had never been comfortable with public speaking, and the idea of having to talk (or worse, making a mistake) in front of his entire class terrified him.

Public speaking is the top fear in the United States, and most people deal with some form of nervousness or anxiety when giving a presentation. If you struggle with public speaking, you are with the majority of students. The general fear around public speaking is, honestly, why your teacher assigns class presentations. A presentation allows you to practice your public speaking skills while also demonstrating your mastery of the topic. The only way you will overcome your hesitancies about public speaking is to practice, so this section will focus on how to help you prepare for your upcoming class presentation.

Structuring an oral presentation

The first thing I tell my students (after telling them not to panic) is to think about class presentations as oral essays. You don't need to invent a whole new organizational style to give a good presentation; instead, you can provide good, easy-to-understand presentations by structuring them like an essay.

Lesson 81: Structure like an essay

If you have prepared a visual aid like a PowerPoint, then you already have a solid structure for your presentation. If you are not using any form of visual support for your presentation, you will need to structure your presentation clearly.

Just like in an essay, start your introduction with an interesting fact about your topic to encourage your audience's genuine attention. Give an overview of the issue and any necessary background information. Then, clearly state your thesis. You should use language that indicates this is the main point of your presentation; use tone and body language to emphasize it. Once you have stated your thesis, briefly outline your main points. It gives your audience an auditory roadmap to your presentation, which is vital for understanding what you're saying.

Now you can go through each point individually. Start with a chronological marker like 'first,' 'second,' or 'third' to help your audience keep track of where you are in your speech. Then, state what the main idea of this point is. Give your evidence, analysis, and evaluation before restating the main idea of this point and how it relates to the thesis of your presentation. Repeat this for every point in your presentation. As you move through your essay, it is important to follow this structure of previewing your point, giving your point, and reviewing your point. Modern audiences do not listen well, so give your audience plenty of reminders about where you are, where you have been, and where you are going in your presentation. This oral structuring is called signposting, and it helps your audience better understand your presentation.

Your conclusion should give your thesis again, review your main points one last time, and end with a sentence or two about how your presentation is relevant to the wider world, whether that be the class as a whole or something about life. Like your introduction, your conclusion should be short. I usually recommend spending about a minute each on these two sections.

As you become more experienced with giving presentations, you will start to shift your presentation structure with your topic. It will make for a more organic formation to your presentation. While you are still learning, though, I recommend sticking to this structure. It will help you learn how to give a clear and organized presentation, and you will naturally begin to branch out as you are ready.

Giving your presentation

Now that you have planned your presentation, you can begin to work through how you will present it. It is usually where my students start panicking, so I've included the tips and advice I give to my students before going into a class presentation.

Lesson 82: Use an Outline

Please do not attempt to give your entire presentation from memory. I strongly recommend that you do not write out your full presentation and memorize it word for word. It is more likely to lead to freezing, especially if you forget something.

Instead, I recommend that you speak from an outline. Your outline should have all your main points, your evidence (especially if any of it is a statistic or a quotation), and cue words to remind you of what you wanted to say in between your main points.

If you are using a visual aid for your presentation like a PowerPoint, that is your outline. If you are not using a visual aid, I recommend writing your outline onto flashcards. Number your flashcards in case they get mixed up, and write one point per card. Of course, this is an estimate. Your flashcard should be easy to read quickly and at an arm's distance, so don't put too much on each card. If you have a quotation or a long section, you should use multiple flashcards. There is no limit on how many flashcards you can use, so use as many as you need.

Lesson 83: Practice beforehand

Before you ever set foot in your classroom, you should practice your presentation. Depending upon your experience and nerves, you should start practicing two to seven days before your presentation. The lower your experience (and the higher your nerves) with public speaking, the longer you should plan to practice.

Practice giving your presentation with your presentation, outline, or notecards. Because you aren't memorizing your presentation word for word, it will be a little different every time you practice. That's okay. Notice what works and what doesn't work well in each practice run and improve your presentation every time you give it.

I recommend practicing with a timer so you know how long your presentation is. I also recommend practicing your presentation in front of somebody else, especially if you struggle to speak in front of people. If you are very nervous, start small. Give your presentations to your pet or your teddy bear. Then, once you have practiced once or twice like that, take the next step. Ask someone you trust to listen to you give your presentation. This type of practice will help you prepare for presenting in front of your classmates, and I have found that repeated exposure decreases public speaking anxiety.

Lesson 84: How to look at your audience

The best policy for looking at your audience is to look them in the eye. Oscillate your gaze around the room to avoid staring any one person down. I usually recommend looking at a different person every 15-20 seconds or every time you move to another section of your presentation.

If you cannot bring yourself to look your audience in the eye, that's okay. Many new public speakers struggle with this. If this is your struggle, then pick two or three people in different areas of the room and alternate between them. Look at their foreheads or their ears. It will give you the semblance of looking at your audience while also managing your nerves about public speaking. As you become more experienced, you may find you don't need to do this anymore. That's good; it means you are becoming more comfortable as a public speaker.

Lesson 85: Remember to Breathe

I know this one sounds obvious, but many people seem to forget how to breathe once they get in front of an audience. Not breathing heightens any uneasiness or nerves you may have felt because your brain isn't getting the oxygen it needs. So, the first thing you should do when you get up to give your presentation is to take a deep breath. It's okay to take three seconds to breathe; I know it might feel awkward for you, but it doesn't feel uncomfortable for anyone else.

Plan in some strategic places in your presentation to take more deep breaths. The end of points is usually a natural spot to breathe, as it is immediately after a long piece of evidence. Use your breaths also to give your audience a few seconds to process what you've been saying. Your pauses are not awkward; if used strategically, they are actually part of a good presentation.

Group Projects

Amanda hates group projects. Every time her teacher would assign a group project, she would come into tutoring, fuming about how unreliable people in her group are and how she never knows how to handle it correctly. I never managed to fully dissuade her of the idea that group projects are inherently evil, but group projects can be a good thing. Group projects are supposed to disperse the weight of a task while demonstrating your understanding of the material. They also help you practice interpersonal relationship skills, which you need for the rest of your life. All you need is an understanding of the material (which your study skills will help with) and some basic rules and etiquette for working with other humans.

Basic Rules and Etiquette

Most of the conflicts, problems, and frustrations that arise from group projects can be fixed before starting with some basic rules and etiquette. While you cannot force everyone in your group to abide by these, you can act with the basic decorum due to your group mates. People tend to respond positively to politeness, so they are more likely to treat you with the same etiquette you treat them, which you can use to make your group project experience more enjoyable.

Lesson 86: Establish clear guidelines

During your first meeting with your group, one of the things you need to do as a team is establish clear guidelines for the group. These guidelines can center around what format your project will take, when and how often your group should meet, and basic expectations for communication. For example, your group might decide that, because your teacher is expecting a group presentation, you all want to build a PowerPoint, meet in the library Monday and Thursday at 6:30 pm, and communicate in a group chat.

Group projects are all about learning how to work with other people, which requires a great deal of flexibility. While you should know what you would like the group to look like, don't come to the group with the guidelines already set. Your groupmates will not appreciate that. Allow the meeting to create the guidelines collaboratively. Of course, if you have a non-negotiable (such as you can't meet on Tuesday evenings because you have work), then you should politely but firmly make it known. Most people want the group project to be as smooth and conflict-free as you do, so they are likely to reasonable if you have a non-negotiable as long as you remain flexible about the rest of the guidelines.

For your records, I recommend writing down your group's guidelines. It will help you later if there are any conflicts or if you forget what days you all are meeting.

Lesson 87: Divide tasks equally

During your first meeting as a group, you should also divide the project amongst the group members. Group projects are generally big and are meant to be completed with the joint collaboration of a team. You shouldn't just do the whole task yourself, and you certainly shouldn't push the entire project onto someone else in the group. Instead, everyone should complete an equal portion of the project; this makes the whole task easier to do when done well.

To divide the project evenly amongst your group:

1. Start by listing everything that needs to be done. You can split this by section or by step,

although I usually recommend dividing the project by parts.
2. With the collaboration of your group, divide the tasks equally amongst the members.
3. Remember, some areas are inherently more time-consuming or detailed than others, so consider that as you split the duties.

It might mean that someone is only doing two sections while someone else is doing four, but the workload for each person should be equal.

I suggest writing down what each person is responsible for during your first meeting. Put the list somewhere that everyone in the group can access. It may be in your group chat, on your shared document, or just making photocopies for everyone. Having a written list of the division of tasks will help if any conflict or confusion arises.

Lesson 88: Be nice

It may sound obvious, but it's the most crucial part of group work. Working with people can be difficult, but you can solve and prevent many of the problems that plague group projects by treating everyone politely. Don't purposely be difficult, and try not to respond to negativity. Instead, use your manners. Listen to people without interrupting them and do your work to the best of your ability. Many of your group project conflicts can be eliminated by treating your group mates with the same respect you want them to treat you with. Group projects are meant to help you practice working with people, so use this time to truly practice.

Troubleshooting

Despite all your best efforts, there will be conflicts in your group projects. Some of these are unavoidable, but a few of them are unsolvable. Don't let friction unravel your entire project; instead, try to resolve the conflict.

Lesson 89: Conflict Resolution

The first step you should take once a conflict arises is to identify what the dispute is. Yes, your teammate might be angry and lashing out, but is she lashing out because she feels overwhelmed or doesn't understand the material? Is she mad because she feels she hasn't been heard? There are many reasons why a groupmate might become angry, but the reason behind the anger is the source of the conflict, not the anger itself. If you can identify the basis of the friction, try to resolve it. Suppose your groupmate hasn't done his portion of the project because he needs help setting up the presentation; teach him how to set it up without berating him as lazy. Criticizing him will only extend the conflict and hurt feelings, but politely guiding him will resolve the dispute.

Sadly, not all conflicts can be solved this way. Some conflicts are conflicts of personality, where two group members simply do not get along well. Such conflicts are difficult to solve, so I usually recommend that my students simply be polite. You don't have to like somebody to be courteous. These conflicts have to be endured for the sake of the project and will be good practice for later on.

There are other types of conflicts that you can't solve. I've been in group projects where someone simply refused the work agreed upon. We tried to resolve the dispute on our own, but that person was not willing to cooperate. I've also been in groups where someone is purposely antagonistic, belittling the other group members and creating a hostile environment. We again tried to resolve the conflict, but that person responded negatively to the request. Such situations are rare, but when they do happen, I suggest you go to your teacher. Your teacher has the authority to help manage any conflict resolution. Suppose someone is truly not participating in the group or is hurting the other members. In that case, your teacher may remove that person from your group or grade the project based on individual effort instead of the final communal product. It is the last resort for the rare conflicts you can't solve on your own, but it's good to have a plan in place in case it ever happens. Most group projects don't have unresolvable conflicts, especially if you follow the basic rules and guidelines for successful group work.

Posters/Multimedia

There is an almost endless variety of special projects your teacher can assign, but most of them fall under the concept of a presentation or a group project. However, there are a couple of project types that differ slightly from the projects discussed above, so we will discuss posters and videos here.

Making Posters

Posters are visual displays that present your whole project at the same time. To prevent information overload, you should organize your poster so people can easily understand it.

Lesson 90: Crafting Your Poster

Put your title and central thesis either at the top or center of your poster so they are easier to find. Then, organize the rest of your information into distinct groups on your poster. You can use pictures, colors, diagrams, and other organizational tools to help people navigate your poster efficiently.

You will most likely be presenting your poster to people as they arrive. You may show your poster to the class, or you may have to stand next to your poster while people walk between all the different displays. The latter is common at academic conferences, especially at the collegiate level. Either way, you will be presenting your poster, so you don't need every word of your presentation written on it; however, you should use more words than you would in a PowerPoint. Your poster should be able to present your basic presentation on its own, so use complete sentences and organizational diagrams. You are there to explain your presentation more in-depth and to answer any questions your audience might have.

Making Videos

As technology continues to become more integral to our daily lives, some teachers assign video creation for projects. If you do not already have a video production platform, your teacher or classmates can help you find one.

Lesson 91: Crafting a Video

Videos focus on the combination of visual and auditory effects. Depending on the exact project assigned, you can either film real-life people and objects or use digital animations. A movie or dramatic interpretation tends to use the former, while a presentation of information can use the latter.

If you are filming a short movie for your class project, take the time to plan what you (and your group) will do. Write a script and discuss what specific shots you want to capture on video before you start filming. The auditory elements (like speech and music) should complement the visual aspects, so experiment with camera angles, lighting, and other aspects of cinematography. For example, you are holding the camera over somebody tends to make them look small, which could show a character's lack of power or self-confidence. The most important part of filming is to try to keep the camera steady because it is easier to watch a video that isn't bouncing.

If you are creating a video presentation, you can structure it like a PowerPoint. Start with your title, and then continue through as if you were planning an oral presentation. Just like with PowerPoints, don't use a lot of words. Video watchers can't read a whole paragraph before the video moves on, so to prevent frustration, use more pictures than words. Pictures are an excellent way of communicating complex ideas and examples, and they are often used in video presentations. Your words should help connect the pictures and give any additional necessary information.

Chapter 6 Review

- Construct your presentation like an essay.
- Don't overcrowd your presentation slides.
- Practice your presentation before you give it.
- Most group conflicts are avoidable with cooperation, group planning, and manners.
- Use complete sentences on your posters.
- Utilize the importance of visuals in your videos.

Chapter 7: Miscellaneous Tips and Lessons

So far, we've examined many of the topics I teach my students. I teach them how to study well, how to write well, and how to present well. However, there are a few lessons that I also teach my students along the way. Achieving your academic goals is about more than just using the best studying methods or sitting in the best seat in class. So, in this chapter, we'll go over the last miscellaneous lessons you need to complete your academic success.

Staying healthy

While academic success may be your goal right now, please remember that your health comes before your goals. You won't be able to achieve anything if you work yourself sick. It was something Amanda really struggled with; she was so focused on getting a better grade that she didn't sleep much and didn't properly handle her stress. Not taking care of herself was hurting her grades and making her sick. Maintaining your health is something I work with all of my students on because you are more important than your grades.

Physical Needs

While you are working through school, you need to maintain your physical needs. It is how you keep yourself from getting sick, which allows you to spend more time succeeding with your goals.

Lesson 92: Please get some sleep

Many of my students come to me sleep-deprived because they have been studying and working so late into the evening that they only have a few hours to sleep. It isn't healthy; your brain needs sleep to process the day properly, and your body needs time to rest and recover. If you don't get enough sleep, you will eventually get sick, leaving you unable to continue progressing towards your goals.

Experts recommend getting around 8 hours of sleep a night, although some people need a little more. If you are trying to get your sleep schedule back on track, start by sleeping for 8 hours every night. You are putting yourself at a disadvantage in the classroom if you deprive yourself of the sleep you desperately need, so make good sleep one of your priorities.

Lesson 93: Eating nutritiously

Eating nutritious food is also something some of my students struggle with. Sitting down to a meal takes time, and the junk food tastes good. While I understand and also prefer a bowl of popcorn to a plate of broccoli, I still urge you to make healthy choices. Healthy food contains the vitamins, minerals, and other nutrients that you need to stay healthy, and depriving yourself of these can also make you sick. Choose healthy food for your meals to feed your brain and body, and let the junk food be treats and occasional snacks.

Lesson 94: Find physical activity

Many students neglect exercise once they are no longer in gym classes, especially if they did not find gym class particularly enjoyable. While you don't need a gym membership to achieve good grades, you shouldn't cease all physical activity. It is good for your muscles to stretch and work, and exercise lets your brain work in different ways. Now, physical activity does not have to be rigorous exercise. You can walk to the library, take the stairs to class, or bike to a friend's house. You can also engage in daily rituals like stretching. These will help your body stay healthier, which will help you achieve your academic goals.

Emotional Needs

While most people understand that they should meet their physical needs, they sometimes don't realize that they have emotional needs too. While taking care of your physical needs can help you take care of your emotional needs, there are a few other things you should do to make sure your emotions (and your brain) are healthy.

Lesson 95: What are emotional needs?

While physical needs are the things you need to do to keep your body healthy, emotional needs are the things you need to do to keep your brain healthy. It includes sleeping and physical activity, but it also has security, stability, and stress management.

Meeting your emotional needs does not mean that you should be happy all the time. However, it does mean that you should be reasonably content and feel secure in your current lifestyle and relationships. Everyone meets their emotional needs differently, so you should take some time to reflect on what things and activities make you feel content, secure, and happy. As long as these things are legal and do not limit the freedoms of anyone else, you should engage in those things.

If you find you are struggling to find contentment or happiness, I suggest you reach out to your doctor or a psychologist. These people are trained to help you, and you may need some help in rebalancing your emotional health. You are actually working to meet your emotional needs by asking for help, so let them help you.

Lesson 96: Dealing with stress

Part of taking care of your emotional needs is handling your stress levels appropriately. You should not be stressed all the time. It will not help you be more productive, nor will it help you achieve long-term academic success. Instead, you should plan stress-reducing activities because reducing your stress will help you think more clearly, learn more efficiently, and earn more success. If you find that you are unable to control your stress levels, I again recommend reaching out to your doctor or a psychologist. It is healthy and normal to ask for help, so don't be afraid to let them help you.

There are various stress-reduction activities, and you should find at least five that work for you. I usually recommend that my students spend time on their hobbies, go hang out with friends, or watch an episode of their favorite TV show. You might find that journaling or hiking helps you control your stress. The most important part of your stress management activities is not to make these activities about school. These few hours throughout the week are not a time for you to catch up on your schoolwork or plan your next paper. These are times for you to enjoy life, strengthen your relationships, and do something other than schoolwork. Doing so will dramatically decrease your stress levels because you have planned to get all your work done while taking care of yourself.

Studying online

Recently, I have had more students pursuing their education online. This learning style does have many benefits—it allows you to have access to great material and teachers regardless of time or distance. Online education is especially popular with non-traditional students working towards a college degree. You can take online classes and still hold down a full-time job without intense scheduling concerns. While online education allows more students to obtain their degrees, it does come with its own unique challenges that must be managed for you to succeed.

Lesson 97: Managing yourself

Online classes do offer more flexibility, but that also means that they don't provide a physical classroom or a set schedule. Many students struggle with the lack of rigidity in the class, and their grades suffer accordingly. Online courses do not provide a schedule, so you will need to make one of your own. Using your planner, set aside time every week to attend your classes. I always recommend having multiple study sessions and designated class time throughout the week if possible because this keeps your brain working on the material you are learning.

Once you have made a school schedule for yourself, stick to it. Your success in the virtual classroom will partially depend upon your dedication, so stick to your plan strictly. It will ensure that you have enough time to learn the material and finish the course with your best work. If you put in the effort to make and keep a schedule, you will be able to achieve your academic goals.

Lesson 98: Teaching yourself

Online education offers students access to more course options, greater flexibility, and a larger variety of material than ever before; however, it also can make traditional teaching more difficult. Your online teacher may record lectures or have virtual class meetings, but your teacher may also assign more readings. Reading has been a traditional way to learn that has transitioned well into the virtual world, so take your readings as seriously as any lecture your teacher may record. In some cases, the readings are the only instruction material you will receive, which means you will be reading it to teach yourself the material.

Of course, many online teachers are available via email to answer any questions you may have. Don't be self-conscious about emailing your teacher over questions from the material. It shows that you are eager to learn, and most teachers enjoy teaching students who want to learn. Recently, however, I have had a few students in online classes whose teachers don't respond to emails or questions. It's frustrating when you have to teach yourself the material if you want to learn it. The first thing I advise my students to do is read the material or watch the recorded lecture again. Examine it to see if you can find the answer to your question. If you still aren't sure after reviewing everything, go to your favorite Internet search engine and type in the keywords of this particular unit or chapter. You will find videos and articles discussing your question because although you are taking online classes, you are not learning without any support. Studying online provides access to many resources that you, as your own teacher, are welcome to use.

Procrastination

When my students tell me about their study struggles, they often identify procrastination as one of their biggest problems. They will usually say something about how if they weren't so lazy or could just do the work, they wouldn't have trouble maintaining good grades. I understand it is a common frustration, but from my experience as a student and as a tutor, procrastination is rarely about laziness. It is usually mismanaged anxiety or stress, causing the student to self-sabotage. You can't truly overcome procrastination by just trying harder because the root of the problem is not a lack of will; it's a fear of failure. Overcoming and managing your procrastination is more about fear and anxiety management than self-motivation.

Lesson 99: Build a support system

If you are struggling with procrastination, the first thing you should do is build a support system. Your support system should consist of two or three people who can hold you responsible for your own goals and deadlines. These people can be a tutor, a good friend, or a teacher you are close to. Choose people who will give you a gentle push to keep going and who will celebrate the small victories with you.

Lesson 100: Make achievable goals

Procrastination often is a sign of anxiety, so to relieve that anxiety, break each project and assignment down into achievable goals. Set deadlines for each of these goals, and then focus only on this particular goal. Focusing on the big project will fuel your anxiety, but concentrating on completing each individual piece should give you a sense of accomplishment that will help you continue to progress. Share your goals and your progress with your support team, so they can help you along the way.

Lesson 101: Take care of yourself

Sometimes procrastination is your body's way of asking for a break. When people are tired, they tend to lose focus and self-motivation. Procrastinating on a simple task may be your body's way of reclaiming the rest it needs. When you find yourself staring blankly at your assignment, do a quick check-in with yourself. See if there is a need that you are currently not meeting. You have been following your study plan all along, so if you find you are tired, then stop for the night. Rest will help you be more productive tomorrow, and trying to force productivity now will create more stress, worsening your procrastination.

Chapter 7 Review

- Strive for 8 hours of sleep a night.
- Plan stress-reducing activities into your schedule.
- You must make and keep your own class schedule when learning online.
- Use the resources on the Internet to teach yourself when you have questions during your online classes.
- Procrastination is anxiety, not laziness.
- Treat procrastination with small goals and a support team.

Chapter 8: Conclusion

I love helping my students be successful.

Zach passed his teacher test, graduated with his bachelor's degree in elementary school education, and is now a teacher at an elementary school 30 miles away from his hometown. He's already teaching his students some of the same study skills that I taught him. Zach has also found that some of these skills apply to life as well.

Amanda passed her algebra class. I worked with her for several years as she navigated other courses and learned everything I could teach her about achieving academic success. She's currently preparing for her ACT and has found that her study habits and test-taking techniques are now paying off. She is also working through an AP track, and she is excited to start college soon.

For me, being a tutor is all about helping my students be successful. Success starts in the classroom with being prepared and actively engaging in your education, but it continues outside the classroom with how you structure your study time, essays, and projects. Being academically successful takes a lot of work, but if you are willing to put in the work, you can be successful too. I hope this book has been a support to you in your academic ventures, and I look forward to hearing all about your successes.

About the Expert

Sarah Fantinel has been a tutor of all ages for five years. She enjoys helping students discover their academic potential and has helped many students improve their grades and pass various standardized tests, including the ACT and the teacher test. Sarah first started tutoring in college because she wanted to help her peers be successful, and tutoring has allowed her to celebrate the little victories of life with her students.

Holding degrees in both English and Humanities, Sarah currently lives in Arkansas with her dog and sixteen-year-old cat. When she is not writing or tutoring students, Sarah likes to take walks and explore new burger restaurants.

HowExpert publishes quick 'how to' guides on all topics from A to Z by everyday experts. Visit HowExpert.com to learn more.

Recommended Resources

- HowExpert.com – Quick 'How To' Guides on All Topics from A to Z by Everyday Experts.
- HowExpert.com/free – Free HowExpert Email Newsletter.
- HowExpert.com/books – HowExpert Books
- HowExpert.com/courses – HowExpert Courses
- HowExpert.com/clothing – HowExpert Clothing
- HowExpert.com/membership – HowExpert Membership Site
- HowExpert.com/affiliates – HowExpert Affiliate Program
- HowExpert.com/jobs – HowExpert Jobs
- HowExpert.com/writers – Write About Your #1 Passion/Knowledge/Expertise & Become a HowExpert Author.
- HowExpert.com/resources – Additional HowExpert Recommended Resources
- YouTube.com/HowExpert – Subscribe to HowExpert YouTube.
- Instagram.com/HowExpert – Follow HowExpert on Instagram.
- Facebook.com/HowExpert – Follow HowExpert on Facebook.

Made in United States
Orlando, FL
11 January 2025

57202556R00076